Listening
to the Future

Listening to the Future

Why It's Everybody's Business

Daniel W. **Rasmus**

with Rob **Salkowitz**

WILEY

John Wiley & Sons, Inc.

Published by John Wiley & Sons, Inc., Hoboken, New Jersey.
Published simultaneously in Canada.

For general information on our other products and services, or technical support, please contact our Customer Care Department within the United States at 800-762-2974, outside the United States at 317-572-3993, or fax 317-572-4002.

Wiley also publishes its books in a variety of electronic formats. Some content that appears in print may not be available in electronic books.

For more information about Wiley products, visit our Web site at http://www.wiley.com.

Library of Congress Cataloging-in-Publication Data:

ISBN-978-0-470-41344-9

Printed in the United States of America

10   9   8   7   6   5   4   3   2   1

Contents

Microsoft Executive Leadership Series: Series Foreword

The Microsoft Executive Leadership Series provides leaders with inspiration and examples to consider when forming business strategies to stand the test of time. As the pace of change quickens and the influence of social demographics, the impact of educational reform, and the impetus of national interests evolve, organizations that understand and embrace these underlying forces can build strategy on solid ground. Increasingly, information technology is bridging social, educational, and international distances, and empowering people to perform at their fullest potential. Organizations that succeed in the enlightened use of technology will increasingly differentiate themselves in the marketplace for talent, raw materials, and customers.

I talk nearly every day to executives and policy makers grappling with issues like globalization, workforce evolution and the impact of technology on people and processes. The idea for this series came from those conversations—we see it as a way to distill what we've learned as a company into actionable intelligence. The authors bring independent perspectives, expertise, and experience. We hope their insights will spark dialogs within organizations, among communities, and between partners about the critical relationship between people and technology in the workplace of the future.

I hope you enjoy this title in the Microsoft Executive Leadership Series and find it useful as you plan for the expected and unexpected developments ahead for your organization. It's our privilege and our commitment to be part of that conversation.

DANIEL W. RASMUS
General Editor, Microsoft Executive Leadership Series

Titles in the Executive Leadership Series:

Rules to Break and Laws to Follow by Don Peppers and Martha Rogers, 2008.

Generation Blend by Rob Salkowitz, 2008.

Uniting the Virtual Workforce by Karen Sobel Lojeski and Richard Reilly, 2008.

Drive Business Performance by Bruno Aziza and Joey Fitts, 2008.

Listening to the Future by Daniel W. Rasmus with Rob Salkowitz, 2009.

Business Agility by Michael Hugos, 2009.

Leading the Virtual Workforce by Karen Sobel Lojeski and Richard Reilly, 2009.

*L*istening to the Future is the product of more than four years of ongoing research, planning sessions, and conversations with customers, partners, policy-makers, and experts. In addition to offering Microsoft's perspective on the future of business and work, it provides a glimpse behind the scenes to explore how the world's leading software company looks at issues beyond technology, and thinks strategically about the landscape that customers will face.

At Microsoft, the scenario planning process is not simply a thought exercise. It is a tool to assist in the development of business strategy, product design, and marketing. Dan has shared many of the ideas in this book with hundreds of customers in executive briefing sessions, leading to deeper levels of engagement and intriguing exchanges. Some customers have used the ideas and methods as springboards for their own internal strategy conversations—not just around software and technology, but in explorations of fundamental issues facing their own business and industry.

Microsoft has published some of this material before, as white papers and as a special-order book. This new trade edition features a vastly revised, extended and refined look at the earlier themes, packaged to appeal to a broad audience interested in the future of business and the future of work. We encourage people to engage with these ideas, argue, question, and challenge them, and in the process, realize some of the benefits that Microsoft has gained from listening to the future.

DANIEL W. RASMUS
ROB SALKOWITZ
November, 2008

Acknowledgments

The authors wish to thank Chris Capossela, Betsy Frost, Sam Hickman, Larry Marion, Lawrence Wilkinson, Liz Longworth, Gigi Villa, Heidi Metz, Bill Roberts, Alice Shimmin, Anna Sprague, Rebecca Alexander, Jan Shanahan, Guy Roadruck, Chris Munson, and the teams at Triangle Publishing Services, MediaPlant LLC, and BuzzBee Company for their input and assistance on this project. Thanks also to Tim Burgard and the editorial and production team at Wiley and Sons for all their support in bringing this book to press.

CHAPTER 1

Listening to the Future

I n ancient times, leaders would perform elaborate sacrifices and rituals
in an attempt to gain some cryptic bit of foreknowledge that might give
them an advantage against rival armies or palace intrigues. The future,
after all, was just one of a great many mysteries that the human intellect
had yet to penetrate. The Ouija board, the Zodiac, or the I-Ching seemed
as good a technology as any to ascertain the unknowable.

Thousands of years of human history have passed, but accurately
forecasting future conditions still requires more art than science. Today
we possess more data about the world, better tools for analysis, and
mature theories about how the universe works, but as these extremely
powerful components come together to highlight trends and explain
complex natural phenomena, they highlight the weaknesses of predic-
tion just as often. Greater data about the universe brings into question
fundamental beliefs about physics. The mapping of the human genome
forces a reevaluation of "junk DNA" as previously hidden connections
and functions are revealed. Economic theories that presupposed the

existence of "rational actors" now increasingly contain footnotes about forecasts as underlying assumptions about behaviors and relationships in the economy shift. Although our interpretation of cause and effect is often accurate, many models still reflect outputs whose origins vary greatly with subtle changes to initial conditions. Despite the limitations of forecasting, we can use our analysis, combined with insight, to identify potential problems years in advance and start formulating policies to address them before they become a crisis; or we can spot opportunities and attempt to arrive at the right place, at the right time, to take advantage of them.

Ironically, it is the vast and growing power of our analytical and observational tools that can cause the most trouble in our efforts to plan for the future. Information breeds expertise. Experts become vested in their positions and confident in their analytical powers. Careers are built on knowing things. As confidence hedges toward certainty, experts and those who listen to them start sketching their visions of the future in heavier lines and more vivid and vibrant colors, until these schematics become so convincing that no other alternatives seem plausible. As a result, the market for futures has come to resemble a Middle Eastern bazaar, crowded with gaudy hawkers crying out their wares:

"Globalization is inevitable and irreversible!"

"No, nationalism and fundamentalism will bring down the global order!"

"Aging populations will doom the developed world!"

"The economy is headed for collapse because of peak oil!"

"Technological innovation is pushing us toward a 'singularity' that will trigger the next phase of human evolution!"

Each of these positions, and dozens of others, has its adherents, armed with reams of data and internally consistent modes of analysis that point inexorably toward their mutually incompatible and wildly contradictory conclusions.

The diversity of expert opinion about the future is worse than useless to business leaders, policy makers, and ordinary people who have to make decisions in the here-and-now based on reasonable expectations of what is to come. At least in the days of séances and sacrifices, the spirits would not argue among themselves about the prophesies they handed down to the faithful. But today, placing a bet on one school of expertise or one convincing method of analysis means placing a bet *against* a score of competing and potentially just-as-likely futures. When the stakes are high, the consequences of leaning the wrong way with unjustified confidence can be disastrous.

EMBRACING UNCERTAINTY

Fortunately, a more humble path can lead to more robust results. For years, many organizations have positioned themselves for success by embracing the concept of uncertainty. That doesn't mean throwing up your hands and saying "I don't know!"—and dispensing with the concept of planning altogether. Rather, it involves sifting through the possibilities, identifying the antipodes of extreme positions, and considering multiple future scenarios instead of one concrete future vision. The goal of the planning process is to identify strategies that are effective and resilient across the widest range of potential futures—not just to hedge bets against unforeseen risks, but to ensure that the organization will be watchful for future events in time to respond with appropriate agility to their forecasted opportunities and contingencies at the lowest possible cost—and with the hope their careful anticipation was more robust than their competitors.

Microsoft's approach to forecasting is modeled on the scenario planning methodology developed by Royal Dutch Shell in the 1970s, and later formalized by the Global Business Network consultancy. Starting in 2003, Microsoft began a series of structured visioning exercises with internal and external groups, including Microsoft employees, customers, partners, and several groups of college-age students (The Information Work Board of the Future) that led to the development of four scenarios, or possible futures, against which we could test ideas about the future of business, technology, and work.

Scenarios start by recognizing the importance of driving forces that will likely shape the new world of work and business: globalization, demographic change, the spread of networks and information technology, the drive toward transparency and regulation, the blending of work and life, and mounting concerns over energy and the environment. These forces are real and are supported by statistics and data, by anecdote and experience, *and* by the weight of expert opinion, as we will explore in later chapters. However, the driving forces by themselves don't predict any certain outcome or set version of the future because they are individual vectors in a complex world. How these forces interact and play out precludes any definitive answer about the future, regardless of how certain we may be of the elements.

Each driving force suggests questions rather than answers. Will globalization continue on its current course, or trigger a backlash of resurgent nationalism and regional conflict? Will aging workers leave the workforce, stick around beyond traditional retirement age, restart careers late in life, or shed the "workaholic" tendencies associated with Baby Boomers throughout their working lives in favor of a more balanced view of work and life? Will networks and technology help large organizations consolidate their power by leveraging their scale, leaving ever smaller opportunities for competitors, or will power shift to nimble players able to collaborate in opportunistic partnerships in a more innovative, dynamic world?

The outcomes of these and other similar questions don't point to one future but to many, each with its own attributes and implications for work and business. The scenario planning methodology helps lay out the possibilities like points on a compass, with the axes determined according to the two most important uncertainties, per the consensus of the planning group(s). At Microsoft, we chose to define our north–south uncertainty axis as the predominant organizing principle of the world: centralized and hierarchical or distributed and networked. The east–west axis is defined by the trajectory of globalization: towards greater global integration or towards a more bordered, regionally focused world. The resulting grid defines four quadrants, each representing a different combination of characteristics—centralized and global, centralized and

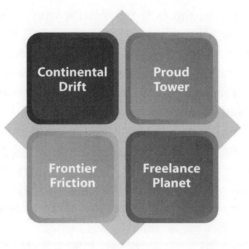

FIGURE 1.1   Microsoft Scenarios

bordered, distributed and global, and distributed and local. Starting with those basic defining qualities, our small teams built up stories around each future scenario, giving each a distinct personality and a distinct name (see Figure 1.1).

Because the poles of the compass represent the most divergent outcomes of critical uncertainties, the scenarios force the reader to accept a new set of logic that is beyond any individual experience or constrained intuition. That is by design. The scenarios create a framework for stories about the future that don't *predict* what will happen, but that create environments that help challenge assumptions, spur creativity, and create a canvas of possibilities that can be monitored.

Although two uncertainties define the scenario matrix, all of the driving forces and the other uncertainties act as characters in the stories about the future. The scenarios gain the richness of logic and direction so that other elements, when played out against these stories (see Four Visions of the Future: Microsoft's Scenarios, below), behave according to the logic of the scenario, and therefore very differently from scenario to scenario. The completion of the stories creates the groundwork for testing assumptions, for exploring the answers to strategic questions, and for asking open-ended questions and seeing where they lead.

Scenarios often recoup their investments within days or weeks of their development because they create a new way of sorting strategic imperatives, starting new projects, or helping shut down projects that prove questionable in light of the scenarios. But scenarios best prove their value over the long-term as entry points for monitoring the future and as a windtunnel for new ideas.

Windtunneling borrows a metaphor from aerospace and automotive design. In traditional windtunneling, air is blown over a design with colored smoke, or in more modern versions, sensors, to help visualize the aerodynamics of a design. Windtunneling has also been used to refine the way ski jumpers hold their bodies and skis for maximum lift. With scenarios, the stories act as windtunnels for ideas, with the narrative blowing over them to see how the design of the idea holds up within the logic of the world. And like traditional windtunneling, an idea that doesn't fare well can be redesigned and retested until it is robust against multiple futures. Ideas can also be deconstructed until certain elements prove their resilience against multiple futures. This helps designers sort out core features, which are robust in all scenarios, from contingent features, which can be added, removed, or modified depending on the direction of future events. It also prevents overinvestment in areas that are most vulnerable to uncertainty and disruptive change.

In Microsoft's case, windtunneling can help ensure that a core set of capabilities envisioned at the beginning of a long product development cycle remain relevant to the needs of customers when the product comes to market, perhaps years later. Although it is not possible to *precisely* predict future business conditions and customer needs, the next best thing is to deliver a product, service, or strategy resilient against different scenarios and contexts, rather than optimizing for one possibility that may or may not actually materialize.

The final purpose of the scenarios is to serve as conceptual guideposts to help make sense of developments in the world. In the corridor outside Dan's office at Microsoft, there is a large bulletin board divided into a four-quadrant grid of the scenarios. Clipped news stories are posted on the board according to which scenario they reinforce. In the Proud Tower quadrant, you might see a *Wall Street Journal* article about the uptick in corporate mergers and acquisitions (M&A) activity, or a piece from *PC World* talking about a new technology for watermarking digital documents. In the upper right ("Continental Drift"), perhaps a story from *The Economist* on the increasing integration of regulation regimes in the EU, or a newspaper editorial advocating increased trade tariffs. Over time, the entire board becomes thickly carpeted with stories, each providing a scrap of evidence for the emergence of one scenario or another. The framework helps us contextualize the constant stream of information and provides early warnings for a swing toward one of the competing poles of uncertainty. It also helps create visceral proof that relying on any one forecast might prove a dangerous assumption.

Although scenario-planning method does not tell us exactly where we are going, it creates a useful frame for conversations and observations, which can then be translated into action. When Microsoft engages in business discussions with customers, the scenarios help define meaningful questions and act as a framework for interpreting the answers. Perhaps most importantly, the scenarios help create a learning dialog about the future priorities and strategies with customers that refines what is important to the market. As Microsoft learns from its customers, the scenarios become ever-richer canvases for strategic conversations.

Four Visions of the Future: Microsoft's Scenarios

SCENARIO 1: PROUD TOWER

Proud Tower describes a future where merger and acquisition activities have led to large, centralized, vertically integrated corporations. These oligopolies have subsumed many of the functions of governments, including education and development of local infrastructure. International laws also favor large businesses and prioritize defense of their intellectual

(continued)

property. Globalization creates a fertile climate for transnational commerce, with economic opportunities leading to rapid development in emerging nations, within the constraints of the oligarch investments. Many companies have created their own security and encryption capabilities because of a distrust of commercially available solutions. Since a few large companies dominate the market, it is difficult for small competitors to gain a foothold. Consequently, companies compete at the margins for market growth and revenue opportunities within their existing customer base, while innovation suffers. Many global revenue models look more like annuities, as products and services both offer support plans that rollout updates or replacements on a regular basis. Workers make their careers by climbing the corporate ladder, building relationships within their organization, and blending their personal lives with the culture and priorities of their employers. Most workers earn a comfortable living and are highly educated through strong K-12 programs and corporate universities.

Some additional characteristics of this scenario include:

- Borders are increasingly fluid, with global corporations as the primary organizing principle of commerce at every level.
- Security and intelligence needs tend to outweigh issues of privacy, and U.S. military and global corporations form increasingly close relationships.
- Corporations pay more attention to issues of governance, accountability, and sustainability, recovering some civic trust. But new global and social tensions are rising as people anticipate the century's third decade, even as economic inequalities continue to widen.
- Highly proprietary, structured, corporate-monitored information systems and networks dominate technology infrastructure. The Internet is primarily a means for connecting to work and a place to interact through highly sponsored and corporate regulated sites.
- Corporations, some of which may deploy proprietary algorithms due to distrust among the companies that offer security solutions, control intellectual property.
- Workers are (and must be) loyal to corporations. The rise of *organization person* becomes the politically correct version of Whyte's 1950s *organization man*.[1] The conformist, approval-seeking aspects

of the Millennial workstyle make them a good fit for this kind of culture.

■ Emphasis is on intra-organizational collaboration and communication as people use information and process expertise to gain status within corporate meritocracies. Internal networking and politics are more important than external relationships.

■ Searching and filtering of internal information proves equally (or more) important than looking for external information as internal efficiencies and consistency drive corporate agendas.

■ Organizationally oriented reputation systems help people figure out the best people inside the organization to work with to achieve their goals.

■ Organizations are worried about information leaking out as a kind of paranoid overprotection in a world where few, if any, could duplicate a capability. Much of the worry about information is due to the opacity of process and the desire to maintain a certain perception and image in the market regardless of actual operating practices.

SCENARIO 2: CONTINENTAL DRIFT

Continental Drift envisions a retrenchment from globalization and a return to competitive nation-states or regional blocs. Political problems have complicated relationships among the United States, Europe, China, and the Middle East, restricting access to manufacturing capabilities, raw materials, overseas markets, and immigrant labor. Although oil remains in adequate supply, the transportation of oil proves ever more risky, with many nations choosing to reduce the length of supply chains, and in many cases, bringing back goods production to national soil. National governments become much more assertive in creating industrial and labor policies, reflecting a return to economic nationalism and a disenchantment with free market and neo-liberal theories that dominated the prior decades. The decline in trade increases the stagnation of the world economy and lowers the levels of wealth-creation. Increasingly ideological governments disdain pragmatic interest-balancing approaches in favor of strident solutions to domestic and international issues. A few large businesses thrive on government contracts and subsidies while competing among themselves for share of domestic markets. Most businesses become increasingly associated with their

(continued)

nation of origin as they pull their edges in toward a more secure, controlled, and predictable core. Some nation-states nationalize industries, eliminating the subsidiaries of multinationals overnight. Political friction rivals that of the Cold War with security measures that make it difficult to do business across borders. Workforce development and education are huge government priorities, and workers in most developed economies have strong leverage in negotiating pay, benefits, and working conditions because of labor shortages caused by demographics, as long as concessions are made to behavior and information requirements within the largely state-controlled labor system.

Some additional characteristics of this scenario include:

- Increasing global problems—terror, economic turmoil, and environmental degradation—lead to the return of big government across the world.

- Though the U.S. remains militarily powerful, a series of strategic missteps significantly weakens its economic and cultural influence relative to rising powers elsewhere in the world.

- Major governments in Europe and Asia raise taxes to pay for large infrastructure projects intended to kick-start a stagnant and more regionalized world economy.

- Regional innovations do not spread globally as the distrust of information causes much duplication of effort, and security barriers at national firewalls often halt the news of regional discoveries until they can be used to political advantage.

- A new generation of young nationalists, particularly in fast-growing economies like China and Brazil, support and spur increasingly confrontational military and economic policies on the part of their governments.

- High regional compliance overhead hamstrings growth as nations promulgate new forms of compliance to keep their local businesses in line and deter international trade except when necessary for survival.

- Differences rule: New local competitors emerge in various regions as the disruption of the global economies creates local niches for businesses once dominated by multinational firms and brands.

- Playing by local rules is as important as (or more important than) efficiency, causing many firms to reduce their profit expectations for business continuity goals, often creating complex relationships to maintain some control over international holdings by fragmenting internal operations to comply with local regulatory demands.

- Being culturally competent and being multilingual are valued skills among employees charged with negotiating the increasingly less penetrable boundaries between nations.

- Emphasis is on interorganizational collaboration and communication with the nation-state creating consortiums of suppliers and services operators to meet the needs of central plans.

- High concern over information boundaries leads many national governments to create strict regulations on the movement of information and investing heavily in filtering and encryption technology to restrict access to national assets.

- As standards fragment and fracture, information translation and format transcription will prove invaluable to maintain fluidity. Much early work done by hand will be automated over time.

- Regionally oriented reputation systems dominate with barriers that exclude finding expertise or managing relationships outside of approved boundaries.

SCENARIO 3: FRONTIER FRICTION

Frontier Friction emerges following a severe shock to the global economic system: perhaps a data meltdown in the financial sector following a cyber-attack. An attack against information generates a general pushback against technology as people lose confidence in the industries that turned their money, and their lives, into the binary language of ones and zeros. Over a very short period of time, confidence in the old order collapses and authority devolves to regional governments, communities, religious sects, and emergent and traditional clan and tribal affiliations. This is a problematic scenario for business. Companies must create and enforce their own security policies and operate in an environment of low trust among employees, customers, and partners. With economic and educational infrastructure in disrepair, the quality of the knowledge workforce continues to degrade, requiring simpler tools and practical skills. Supply chains are fragmentary if they exist at all, and much of the economy becomes localized, with networks of communities interrelating at the near-local level.

(continued)

Some additional characteristics of this scenario include:

- Power and influence seep away from hierarchical institutions and corporations, as the old rules stop working and citizens tear down working institutions out of fear and distrust.
- Facing a dynamic and dangerous world, people crave a sense of belonging and focus on communities and relationships; this gives rise to fundamentalism as well as new "swarm" models of communities that assemble and congregate based on current needs rather than long-term thinking.
- Privately funded nonprofits and nongovernmental agencies step in to fill many of the functions of governments starved of resources and crippled by corruption.
- The distrust of all centralized political or social entities heightens the importance of individual security and individual validation of truth.
- Individuals see a need for multiple aliases as they navigate across tribal boundaries, while simultaneously demanding stringent background checks and checkpoints for new entrants to a community.
- Burgeoning youth populations in the world's poorest countries, and among the world's most insular religious sects, generate increasing intolerance, social disorder, and violence. Job skills decline among younger people and many industries are threatened with serious labor shortages.
- The maintenance of older products becomes equally as lucrative as shipping new products as the adoption rate of innovation crawls and people reuse and reapply existing technologies and tools to new problems.
- The ability to move between networks and make new partnerships is crucial as local resources are often very scarce and insufficient to meet needs.
- Translation skills—at every level and in every way—are at a premium as the fragmentation of the world creates new social and cultural pockets that begin to evolve independent systems, even languages, that force the need for people who can navigate through their information and cultural boundaries.

- Information distrust is very high, leading to much missed information. This further enhances ignorance and reinforces insular behavior.
- Home schooling or religious schooling predominates the education environment.
- Community-oriented reputation systems that key off *very* trusted sources are one of the few community applications that remerge as valuable to the new, isolated communities.

SCENARIO 4: FREELANCE PLANET

Freelance Planet is a world transformed by bottom-up networks and mass collaboration on a global scale. The flexibility and speed of networked systems renders centralized command-and-control hierarchies obsolete at all levels. Large corporations become holding companies and managers of relationships between independent contractors and small providers. Governments outsource and devolve their functions to entrepreneurial nonprofits and nongovernment organizations. People seamlessly blend their lives and work, managing multiple identities, networks, and overlapping relationships using technology that pervades every device and environment. Rapid innovation and creative thinking are competitive advantages. People and businesses invest continuously in learning. New hotspots of creative thinking flare up unpredictably all around the world, creating global attention deficit disorder as most people find it hard to sort out what will be important today, let alone tomorrow. Workers manage their own savings and their own healthcare, or join one of the many guilds or associations that attract people who require a sense of physical community in the ever more fluid and impersonal world of business.

Some additional characteristics of this scenario include:

- Network, speed, and creativity rule. Traditional hierarchies become increasingly ineffectual, as emergent systems succeed in surprising new ways, including distributed intelligence networks that greatly enhance security.
- Voices of the previously disenfranchised enjoy growing influence; even so, a rapidly changing technological society is challenging to many institutions and people.

(continued)

- More expertise is available online so people create just-in-time learning opportunities, further eroding any hope for the few remaining businesses built on proprietary practices or intellectual property.

- There is increased emphasis on relationship management in all aspects of life, and across "outsourced" borders. People have massive contact lists that are tagged to help locate the right people for the right problem (contacts become contextual).

- Information security moves off the network and the operating system to the object, completely shifting security expectations. Network penetration and operating system hijacking result in interesting experiments but do little to compromise the information encapsulated in content containers, some of which have very protective behavior shells that limit access to their contents.

- A general blurring between enterprise and extra-enterprise networks exists with new security software in play that quickly analyzes objects on a device attached to a network and isolates any threats while allowing the user to connect to authorized data and applications. This development precipitates very open networks and drives closer collaboration among partners and customers.

- Strength and success in open innovation leads to the rapid development of new business models, new businesses, and new products and services.

- The short half-life of success means that many start-ups fail in half the time it took previous waves of innovation to be displaced in the market.

- The experience growing up in the rapid-fire, tech-saturated world of the 1990s serves next-generation workers well, as they come to the workforce with strong skills in collaboration, entrepreneurial instincts, and expectations of dynamic change and transparency.

- Schools are reinvented as open institutions with physical locations acting as education hubs for multiple generations and the Internet providing just-in-time anyplace learning of core topics and extended topics constrained only by the pace of the learner.

- Surveillance is highly distributed and often personal, with individual concerns driving how much peripheral vision is employed. Businesses and governments both gather terabytes of video and audio data on a daily basis for later analysis should any law enforcement or regulatory concern require the recall of that information.

■ Popular spiritual movements help people stay connected to each other in some way other than electronically.

■ Computer viruses are rampant, but not as lethal because they are often used as calling cards and proof points for freelancers looking to be hired.

■ Aggregate wealth increases rapidly but is unevenly distributed. Localized boom-bust cycles come and go quickly based on innovation-learning-adoption curves.

■ Very little loyalty remains between employees or employers. Many people work for more than one organization, and most organizations negotiate nonbinding agreements with employees. Some guilds and associations formed around scarce skills negotiate longer term, more binding contracts that cover classes of workers, but not necessarily the individual (e.g., the company agrees to employ fifteen graphic designers—it does not specify which designers, but what class, which also defines skill requirements and pay).

■ Personal prioritization and attention management are the hot software categories as people use software to help figure out what is important and help maintain balance in their lives.

■ People lose their distrust of cloud-based information providers, leading the way to global identification systems that span the breadth and depth of the global talent pool.

THE SHAPE OF THINGS TO COME

Listening to the Future is the distillation of Microsoft's efforts to think about the future of business and work—the challenges and opportunities facing organizations, the transformations that will ripple through the political, economic, and social environments, and the implications for different industries. The scenario work provided a way to test ideas, and the best and most resilient of those ideas are explored here in depth.

In the first part of the book, we investigate four central challenges of doing business in the second decade of the 21st century:

1. **Managing a Dynamic Business:** What are the changes in markets and business models that will shape the future landscape, and how can businesses make themselves resilient?

2. **Prospering in a Blended World:** How can large organizations thrive in an environment of unprecedented diversity in the workforce, the marketplace, and the IT landscape?

3. **Gaining Insights from Complexity:** How can businesses transform the flood of data into useful intelligence to drive decision-making?

4. **Building Strategic Advantage Through IT:** How can the right investments in software and systems help organizations compete in a world where requirements and processes change continuously?

From these four themes of change, the book pivots to a discussion of several factors that are shaping the work experience from the perspectives of the employer, the employee, and parties interested in workforce development and productivity, such as governments, educators, non-government organizations, consumer groups, and industry associations. We have grouped the themes into four main topic sections:

1. **One World of Business:** The drive toward globalization, its implications and consequences, and the role of people and technology in a more integrated global labor market.

2. **Always On, Always Connected:** How pervasive networks and mobile devices are reshaping our understanding of the workplace and workday, and the new set of choices facing people and businesses that arise from an expanded set of possibilities.

3. **Transparent Organizations:** As the costs of opacity grow increasingly unsustainable in a world of constant information and conversation, will the pressure for transparency come from the top down (through regulation) or from the bottom up, via community pressure and new technologies?

4. **Workforce Evolution:** How demographic change, new approaches to education and training, and the diversity of backgrounds and perspectives in the global workforce are challenging workers, managers, educators, and governments.

Knowledge and Talent in the New World of Work brings all of the elements to bear on a single problem: the renewed recognition that knowledge capture, learning, and collaboration will be a major competitive differentiator in a world where high percentages of skilled workers will retire over the coming decades, a world where their successors may not be interested in learning the skills of older workers leaving the workforce, and a world in which ever increasing amounts of work are distributed, along with the knowledge and skills to support that work.

Finally, the book examines various industries, including manufacturing, financial services and insurance, retail, professional services, government and public sector, and healthcare, through the lens of our scenario framework, identifying how the key themes of the new world of work and business might play out in those segments of the economy.

TECHNOLOGY AND THE CHANGING WORLD

Information and communication technology (ICT) is both the means and the motive for many of the changes that have swept over the world in the past 20 years, and new innovations in ICT will help people and organizations manage the changes that are to come. As part of our work, we track the development of new innovations in ICT that may just be appearing on the long-range radar—as research projects, demos, or pilot programs—and think about how they might be incorporated into the mainstream applications that people will use at work in the next 10–20 years. Some of the technologies we are watching include:

- Contextual collaboration
- The evolution of devices
- Interfaces and user experiences
- Machine learning

- Metadata for physical objects and environments
- Modeling and simulation
- Pattern recognition
- Reputation systems
- Smart content and metadata
- Social computing and consumer-generated content (see IT Innovations Shaping the New World of Business below for brief descriptions of these technologies)

Developments in any of these areas are as likely to surface in consumer applications such as Web services, electronic devices, or videogames, as in work or enterprise environments. In fact, if the experience of the past decade is any indication, popular innovations in the consumer economy and uptake by workers will lead enterprise IT planners—sometimes kicking and screaming—to the discovery of the business value of these new tools, rather than vice versa.

While the speed and direction of ICT innovation is itself an uncertainty in the new world of business, it is a theme that plays across all the scenarios. Technology alone does not create and cannot solve the complex challenges of the new world of business, but technology can be deployed strategically to empower businesses to choose the right things to do, and allow them to do them at a place and time that balances the needs of the organization with the needs of the worker and the consumer. Being smart and strategic about the way we use ICT in work and business can also help us avoid creating new problems as we solve old ones—the "two steps forward, one step back" dilemma that usually accompanies rapid change.

IT Innovations Shaping the New World of Business

Contextual collaboration: The different modes of communication and collaboration, including everything from e-mail and instant messaging to social networks and blogs, are still largely isolated, standalone applications that require people to leave one work context and enter another one (e.g., leave a document to go to a shared workspace). However, many vendors are starting to make collaboration capabilities available as Web services, which can be integrated into customized environments and applications based on each user's role and workstyle. As these efforts mature, collaboration and communication will become easier to use and manage for workers and IT, making possible more connected and transparent work practices.

The evolution of devices: Every day yields promising new developments across the spectrum of hardware and devices, from ultra-bright, thin high-resolution displays to long-life fuel cell batteries for notebooks and mobile computers. Communication and computing continue to converge in the form of powerful portable devices that combine telephony, data networking, media recording and playback, information applications, and access to enterprise data. The $100 laptop program is helping to close the digital divide in emerging economies, and this trend will only accelerate as hardware continues to become more powerful, more eco-friendly, and less expensive.

Interfaces and user experiences: For most of the PC era, the keyboard and mouse have provided the primary mode of interaction with computers, and the desk-mounted monitor and printer the primary output devices. Now we are seeing new modes of capturing and outputting data arriving in the workplace, often via the world of videogames. Data gloves, three-dimensional joysticks, and position-sensing devices are joining pens and tablets as alternative ways to input, navigate, and manipulate data; voice-based input is becoming more common and more accurate; smart conference cameras automatically swivel to the person speaking. Software-based interfaces are becoming more immersive, extending to 3D multiuser environments like SecondLife. New wide-screen displays, data surfaces, and digital paper provide alternative means of displaying video data, while 3D printers are coming into wider use for prototyping, product design, and manufacturing. Many of these innovations will find their way into the workplace over the next 10–12 years, bridging the physical gap between people and information.

Modeling and simulation: Now that we are collecting and distributing data in quantities far beyond the ability of the human mind to comprehend, we need ways to abstract and represent that data in a useable format so it can be acted upon. Modeling tools are now starting to enable people to overlay (or "mashup") data from different sources into customized views to reveal

(continued)

hidden relationships. For example, sales data from internal systems can be plotted onto satellite maps from public Web sites and weather information from meteorological agencies to show how weather conditions influence sales of particular items across different regions. Simulation tools enable people to test hypothetical conditions against real-world data to conduct tests of prospective products and services, or perform regression analysis on statistical data to isolate relevant factors.

Machine learning: Machine learning refers to the capability of software to modify the way it behaves based on observation of user preferences or external conditions. Machine learning is used today in self-healing hardware systems and applications that diagnose and troubleshoot problems and either alert IT or fix it themselves. The same kinds of capabilities can be used to create adaptive interfaces that configure themselves based on the workstyles of individual users. Dictation and natural language recognition programs also use machine learning to recognize and adapt to the voice mannerisms of their users.

Metadata for physical objects and environments: Radio-frequency iden-tification (RFID) tags have become a cheap and pervasive way to track physical inventory. RFID and successor technologies such as smart-dust, environmental sensor networks, and surveillance systems that integrate facial recognition and other forms of intelligence, will make it easier to blur the boundaries between the physical and the virtual world. Physical objects can be tracked like data in a network, removing many elements of risk and uncertainty from supply chain management and logistics.

Pattern recognition: Statistical algorithms enable computers to infer re-lationships from complex or incomplete data, simulating the intuition that people use to make sense of words that are missing letters, for example. Improved pattern recognition will help software and interfaces become "smarter," less intrusive and more context-aware, as well as enabling bet-ter natural language capabilities and implicit security policies that do not require passwords. The current limits of pattern recognition software can be seen in the changing styles of the random letter-number-symbol secu-rity codes sometimes required to sign up for Web sites, used to screen out automated sign-in programs. As pattern recognition gets better, the security codes need to become more "fuzzy" and abstract to fool the intruders.

Reputation systems: Reputation systems allow people to rate and tag content such as blog posts or documents in a repository, or the quality of a process. The reputation score is aggregated and visible to everyone else, making high- and low-quality content immediately obvious. Reputation systems are also used by e-commerce sites such as online auctions to help build trust into anonymous transactions by letting trading partners see the past reputations of the people they are dealing with. The use of reputation systems is already spreading to non–Web-based transactions (such as Angie's List service, which assigns reputations to building trade contractors based on user input) and the methods for assigning reputation will become easier and more implicit.

Smart content and metadata: Metadata describes the content of the data it is attached to, such as an ID3 tag associated with an mp3 file that contains artist, album, track number, and so on. Static metadata requires that search engines or databases provide a superstructure of organizing principles (business rules) to locate and organize content (e.g., sorting a music library by artist, then by album, then by year). Smart content is described by *dynamic* metadata that can update itself based on evolving conditions. For example, the metadata of a smart document might include not just the author, date created, date modified, etc., but also a constantly updated list of people to whom it was e-mailed, terms that discovered it in a search, number of times it was printed, and other information including security permissions. Smart content can improve search and content management, help keep documents up to date automatically, and enable content-level security.

Social computing and consumer-generated content: Over the past several years, enterprises have begun to discover the business value of social computing applications that originated in the consumer world, such as blogs, wikis, and social networks. These types of systems are evolving every day, and new channels are starting to extend to social experience to mobile devices via short message service and micro-blogging. These developments will continue, and end-users, particularly younger workers, will likely be out in front of IT departments through grassroots adoption. It will be an ongoing challenge for organizations to rationalize new social computing applications into existing business and IT frameworks, and adopt business practices and culture to a world with permeable boundaries between work and personal life.

PEOPLE MAKE THE FUTURE

The early information age saw large-scale enterprise systems deployed to gather system data and automate business processes. While automation and data collection still deliver value, further refinements to these capabilities will yield only marginal gains. The important innovations of the next decade will come not from large backend systems, but from workers and consumers taking control of data and processes to gain insight into the organization, its customers, and its infrastructure so that new paths to value can be realized.

As social computing and mass collaboration make their way into enterprise environments from the consumer marketplace, they are creating turbulence in work practices and culture: The walls of the enterprise have become more and more permeable, collaboration extends beyond employees to partners, customers and external colleagues, and the free-form communication expectations of sophisticated "digital natives" are clashing with more traditional approaches to work. Blogs, wikis, instant messaging, interactive multimedia, subscription-based content, remote and mobile computing, social networks, content filtering, mashups, and all the other accoutrements of the Web 2.0/ Enterprise 2.0 toolset are redistributing power from centralized hierarchies to the network, changing the way decisions are made, and affecting processes, technology investments, and the shape of the workforce itself.

The latest technologies challenge long-held assumptions about the governance role of ICT as it distributes control to end users and blurs the boundaries between organizations and the broader Internet. Combining business intelligence from consumer platforms with internal data, or deploying collaborative cocreation innovation sites with customers, is not like retooling an assembly line. There is no mechanical equivalent for the closely held relationship between people, process, and information that constitutes today's business environment. Concentrating on data and automation may reduce costs and drive efficiencies, but industrial age models applied to knowledge economy companies will prove crippling and ultimately counterproductive.

The future is far from certain, which is why it is more robust to develop agile, responsive, and fluid business models, and to deploy the technologies to support them, than it is to create rigid, inflexible systems. As history frequently demonstrates, it is easier to reinstate rigidity than to unleash agility.

That dynamic is playing out today as consumer expectations of computing overwhelm the industrial age approach to information. The book is about transition. It points toward new frameworks for business while recognizing the need to move toward new futures as they unfold. In some cases those moves will be cautious, such as when it comes to protecting personal information. Other times, they may be dramatic, such as when it comes to creating new forms of open innovation.

No matter which future unfolds, technology will be a factor in shaping that future, and will provide the tools to help organizations and individuals navigate through the change. This book represents a marker along the journey toward the future, one that we hope proves useful as an input to minimizing risk and discovering the opportunities that will face us all in the new world of business.

NOTE

1. W. H. Whyte, *The Organization Man* (New York: Doubleday, 1956).

CHAPTER 2

Managing a Dynamic Business

Evolving business models, emerging markets, changing customer expectations, and new regulations make it imperative for organizations to become more dynamic so they can remain competitive in a fast-moving and uncertain global marketplace. As these external forces play havoc with convention, organizations need better tools, practices, and technology to help them rapidly adapt to unexpected changes while maintaining their competitive position. Businesses can capitalize on unforeseen opportunities by empowering employees in various ways: to better manage exceptions; to delight customers with exceptional service; and to maintain controls where business continuity and regulatory compliance require them.

DRIVING FORCES

Challenges driving dynamism in the global marketplace over the next ten years include:

Global integration, with the emergence of new markets, new sources of innovation and competition, and the complexities of regulatory compliance in an interconnected global economy.

Emergent business models, including mass collaboration and transparency in product development, disintermediation (cutting out the middlemen) and its effect on the value chain, and the rise of niche markets and high-value customers as profitable alternatives to conventional mass-market approaches. Innovation in emerging markets will reshape channel rules, create new delivery models, and combine services and products into new packages.

Rising customer expectations, driven by consumer experience on the Web and e-commerce, trust and transparency issues, and the use of data to deliver personalized service.

Global Integration

Networks are becoming ubiquitous and pervasive in the majority of economically active areas. Some 22 percent of the world's population had Internet access as of July 2008, according to Internet World Stats (see Figure 2.1, World Internet Usage).[1] Although many rural areas remain without direct Internet connections, these areas increasingly have access to cellular and satellite technology, which in turn provides access to information, processes, and people, and essentially leapfrogs traditional wired services.

Outsourcing comes full circle

The outsourcing of high-value work is now coming full circle, as innovators in emerging markets are establishing operations in developed

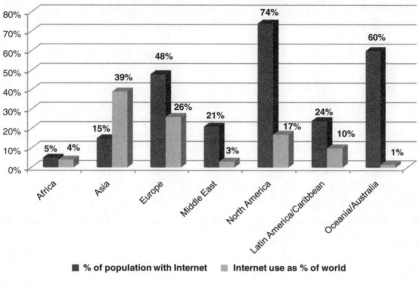

FIGURE 2.1 World Internet Usage

Source: www.internetworldstats.com

economies (see Figure 2.2, Indian Outsourcing Firms Go Global). In-fosys, the India-based IT services company, is already noting that rising wages for programmers, currency valuations, currency, and companies' need for workers in their clients' time zones or who speak languages other than English are challenging the model that jobs can be done cheaper in India (see Thriving in Local Markets).

Company	International Locations
Infosys	China, Czech Republic, Mexico, Thailand
Tata Consultancy Services	Brazil, Chile, Mexico, Uruguay
Wipro	Canada, China, Portugal, Romania, Saudi Arabia

FIGURE 2.2 Indian Outsourcing Firms Go Global

Source: Giridharadas, Anand. "India Tries Outsourcing its Outsourcing." *International Herald Tribune,* September 24, 2007

Thriving in Local Markets

Korean electronics manufacturer LG first set up a factory in India in 1997. Today, its market share is 30 percent, twice as much as its nearest competitor. LG attributes this success to the company's management of its employees, citing an attrition rate that dropped from 19 percent to 6 percent between 2006 and 2008 (the industry average is 35 percent).

LG India executives were allowed to create their own management style, rather than adhering to LG's global style. Because of the competition for good employees, the company made sure that it understood each employee's chosen career path, and then kept them engaged and empowered. Even employees with just a two-year degree in business administration were allowed to make decisions, which few if any other multinational companies in India allowed. The LG India executives' tactics for empowering employees was so well received by the parent company that they are now being taught in other LG offices throughout the world.

Source: http://knowledge.wharton.upenn.edu/india/article.cfm?articleid=4285

The uncertainties of globalization

The complex dynamics of globalization create uncertainty for businesses. No one can say for sure whether current free trade policies will continue to expand, whether political turmoil or supply shocks in energy and commodities will derail the growth of emerging economies, or whether domestic concerns in developed markets will lead to a new wave of protectionism. At the moment, issues such as product safety, customer privacy, market opacity, and corporate governance are driving momentum toward new regulations.

This dynamic, a reversal of the more laissez-faire economic optimism of the 1990s, has driven several years' worth of defensive, compliance-driven IT investments. Will the momentum for top-down regulation continue, or will the next set of pressures come from some other external development? Companies that lay big bets on one particular outcome but then lack the flexibility to adapt to unexpected developments may find themselves in a permanently reactive mode, while more agile competitors move forward by taking advantage of the opportunities that change creates.

Emergent Business Models

The transformative impact of the Internet and a new generation of social computing technologies are profound and ongoing. During the past decade, these innovations have enabled people and organizations to share information, collaborate on projects, and build virtual communities, irrespective of time and geography. In the process, they have made command-and-control hierarchies unnecessary as mediating mechanisms for the flow of information. Organizations are only beginning to come to grips with the impact of the Internet and other technologies on core business functions such as product development, sales, customer relationship management (CRM), and operations.

Collaborative innovation

Many businesses are using networks to bring stakeholders such as customers, suppliers, and outside experts into the product and service development process at an early point. They are replacing the best guesses of designers and marketing experts with quantitative market data and direct customer input.

For example, after leading mobile handset maker Nokia's first media and gaming phone received less-than-stellar reviews in 2003, the company asked its customer base of over one billion to share their ideas on future mobile products and services. "The ability to include large numbers of users in the development cycle means you can have a much more collaborative approach to development and you can try ideas out, refine them, and move forward—or fail fast and get out," said a Nokia spokesperson.[2]

This process of open innovation can reduce the risks and increase the quality of product development, and it makes companies more responsive to their market (see Global Collaboration). However, open innovation requires a different management approach than traditional top-down methods, including incorporating feedback quickly and embracing the idea that innovation is ongoing and never actually finished.[3]

Global Collaboration

McCann Worldgroup is one of the world's largest marketing communications companies. Spanning 130 countries, it represents some of the world's leading firms. A single initiative requires services ranging from initial planning, research, and market analysis to creative execution, media buying, sponsorships, events, and global campaign and brand management. To create global marketing campaigns for its international clients, McCann's geographically dispersed business units must work together within and across all these disciplines.

McCann's employees needed to be able to find colleagues with specific expertise among its seven separate business units. They also needed to search and share content across multiple networks. By deploying collaboration capabilities including search, portal, and content management, McCann Worldgroup now provides its various business groups, project teams, partners, and clients with the ability to collaborate more effectively, to find and share content more easily, and to manage workflows more productively.

Disintermediation of sales and service

Sales organizations across a range of industries are challenged by another effect of networks: disintermediation. Customers not only buy direct anywhere, anytime, over the Web, but also comparison-shop, review case studies and independent data, consult trusted friends and colleagues, and even access unfiltered (and potentially prejudicial) information from blogs. At the same time, companies must understand that the entire sales process is much more information-driven and that individual sales transactions can be improved based on information about a customer's past behavior or information inferred from similar customers. The transaction and resulting customer relationship become not just about what and who the salesperson knows, but about what the enterprise knows and can deliver to the point of sale in terms of customized service.

The increasing viability of niche markets

Networks have deconstructed the notion of the mass market by making it cost-effective for companies to engage with highly segmented and specialized customer groups. They can now profit from items far lower down the inventory power curve (the old 80/20 rule, where 80 percent of volume was generated by the top 20 percent of the catalog) than was previously practical. Writer and analyst Chris Anderson calls this the "Long Tail," and he has argued persuasively that an aggregation of highly loyal niche markets can be more valuable than a mass audience that is easily poached by lower cost competitors.[4]

The rise of emerging market competitors

The sharp and continuing surge of the economies of emerging markets has created a cadre of hungry and skilled competitors (see Figure 2.3, Faster Growth for Developing Economies). Growth in countries such as China and India has led to an increasing number of acquisitions by firms in emerging markets. India's Tata, for example, recently acquired Ford subsidiaries Range Rover and Jaguar.[5] This trend will put pressure on firms to maintain profitability within operating units. It will also increase the monitoring required to understand the competitive landscape.

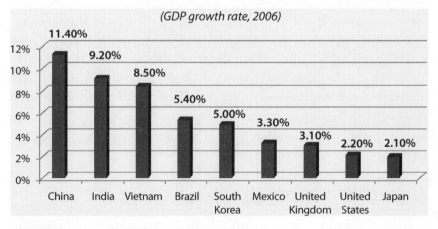

FIGURE 2.3   Faster Growth for Developing Economies

Source: CIA World Factbook, 2007

In addition, changing business models will force organizations to reevaluate their assumptions about sales and support; the integration of operations with external information technology; and the location of warehousing, manufacturing, and distribution centers as costs and capabilities fluctuate with the changing nature of the host countries' economies and labor markets. Executives and managers will have to understand the behavior of their markets to rapidly adapt, and that requires a deep understanding of data and the correlations between data.

Rising Expectations from Customers

The consumer experience on the Web is driving customer expectations of not just e-business but all business, and in both business-to-business and consumer markets. Customers will soon insist on accessing information and digital-based products on demand, anywhere, anytime. Search engines, social computing, and instant messaging make people and data available at a click. Internal processes are exposed as self-service applications on the Web, providing customers with visibility into the status of their package delivery, insurance claim, service request, or parts order. Sophisticated CRM systems help companies offer a highly customized, personal sales and service experience because they know so much about their customers.

The flip side to consumer engagement in innovation is the emergence of "consumer vigilantes," who vehemently engage organizations on issues ranging from product quality and safety to environmental issues and foreign labor policies.[6]

As a result, organizations will have to effectively balance their relationships with consumers and other stakeholders. The multiple channels of the Internet mean that firms will have the ability to keep their customers informed, share critical information with them, and cocreate products, processes, and services.

STRATEGIC TECHNOLOGY CAPABILITIES

Information technology can help people and organizations act quickly to adjust business models, meet rising customer expectations, and roll with the changes in the global business climate. IT helps people manage a dynamic business in the following three important ways:

1. **Connecting people, process, and information** so that people can identify and act on insights more quickly and work together productively to drive change.
2. **Enabling e-business** by facilitating the rapid design and management of rich, interactive Web sites and providing software-based access to shared processes and data.
3. **Providing flexible solutions for changing business needs**, including real-time enterprise management, visibility into supply networks, compliance, and reporting.

Connecting People, Process, and Information

The work that supports rapid change and innovation often happens outside the structured processes supported by monolithic information systems. Routine information tasks, such as managing document life cycles, organizing meetings, sending out notifications of project status, and keeping deliverables current, can consume valuable hours of workers whose expertise would be better applied to tackling new opportunities. Furthermore, optimizing the performance of teams requires software that supports unstructured collaboration. These capabilities include real-time communication, team/individual workflows, self-provisioning team workspaces, wikis, and enterprise e-mail that support information rights management. A dynamic business cannot afford to have every new workspace or content repository shuffled back to IT for approval, so it is critical that the infrastructure deployed to support the business allows individual and team control over how it is deployed and applied.

Finding and using information

Enterprise search is another capability that improves both the quality and the efficiency of teamwork. Studies show that people (knowledge workers) spend as much as 35 percent of their time looking for information and only find what they are looking for 50 percent or less of the

Preliminary research suggests that approximately 35–50 percent of the information available within an enterprise is not centrally indexed. This information resides in databases and desktop or notebook computers. As a result, large or midsize companies can lose millions of dollars per year in lost productivity, based on the following assumptions:

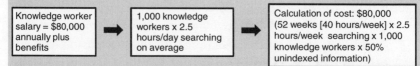

| Knowledge worker salary = $80,000 annually plus benefits | ➡ | 1,000 knowledge workers x 2.5 hours/day searching on average | ➡ | Calculation of cost: $80,000 (52 weeks [40 hours/week] x 2.5 hours/week searching x 1,000 knowledge workers x 50% unindexed information) |

Conclusion: An enterprise employing 1,000 knowledge workers wastes $48,000 per week, or nearly $2.5 million per year, because of an inability to locate and retrieve information. In the aggregate, the 1,000 largest companies could waste at least $2.5 billion per year because of an inability to locate and retrieve information.

FIGURE 2.4   The Cost of Information Not Found

Source: IDC

time (see Figure 2.4, The Cost of Information Not Found).[7] Enterprise search exposes information from multiple repositories, such as shared files, workspaces, enterprise systems, e-mail, and document libraries, in a single view so that people can find the information (and the people) they are looking for more quickly and easily. For structured data, advances in business intelligence mean providing greater access to insight. This insight increases the likelihood that an organization's workers can find new patterns in operations data, customer behaviors, or financial management that will lead to reduced costs, improved efficiency, or a new opportunity for growth (see Achieving Organic Growth).

Achieving Organic Growth

In 2003, Praxair, a Fortune 300 global producer of industrial gases based in Danbury, Connecticut, ambitiously decided to increase revenue by $2 billion in five years. Half of the growth would come from acquisitions, but the other half would require double-digit organic growth of at least $200 million per year. That figure far exceeded the company's annual growth from repackaging helium, hydrogen, oxygen, and other gases.

Praxair executives broke down the company's goals into smaller, more actionable categories. They estimated that the first 15 percent would come from incremental growth in its base business, in addition to new channels serving current markets. The rest would have to come from new services for new industries. Praxair was successful in these initiatives—it achieved $230 million in growth in 2004—because the company had intimate knowledge of its customers' changing needs and its executives understood how to meet those needs with Praxair's current capabilities.

Source: http://knowledge.wharton.upenn.edu/article.cfm?articleid=1662&CFID=71034356&CFTOKEN=25041277

Collaborating around business data

Insights from business intelligence, project management reporting, and a variety of other information sources, have more value if they are part of a collective conversation about how to achieve an organization's goals and objectives. Data must be openly available and easily integrated into a collaboration environment so that workers can take action on it. Similarly, the insights resulting from studying this more readily available data must also be made accessible for collective use. Doing so completes the virtuous circle of increased access leading to measurable results.

Consistent, contextual collaboration

When the facilities for team collaboration are based on an enterprise platform rather than a piecemeal set of freestanding applications, it becomes much easier to improve performance across organizational groups, outside vendors, customers, and other stakeholders without incurring huge IT services costs. With an enterprise collaboration platform in place, businesses can more easily adapt to new models, facilitate innovation, and integrate feedback from customers to meet competitive demands.

Enabling E-Business

E-business remains the focal point of change in nearly all industries, even as we move beyond the basic transactional capabilities of e-commerce. Popular sites like YouTube, Facebook, Twitter, and other examples of

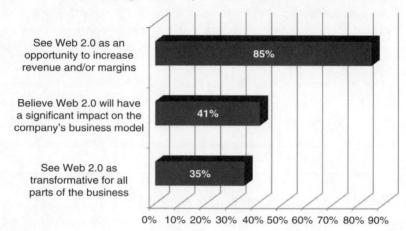

According to a survey of 406 C-level executives worldwide:

FIGURE 2.5   CXOs Optimistic About Web 2.0
Source: The Economist, 2007

Web 2.0 approaches are driving consumer expectations for transparency, immediacy, and interactivity, and they are forcing companies to adapt to a new set of conditions, especially in the areas of sales, marketing, and customer service (see Using Web 2.0 to Transform a Bad Situation). According to a survey by *The Economist*, 85 percent of C-level executives see Web 2.0 as an opportunity to increase revenue or margins (see Figure 2.5, CXOs Optimistic About Web 2.0). Every company must decide on its own strategy to meet these challenges, but the common requirement is an extensive, secure technology platform that enables rapid development of new Web-based applications.

Using Web 2.0 to Transform a Bad Situation

Companies should not panic in the face of social networking. While they can no longer rely solely on one-way messaging that they control, companies should recognize the potential benefits in these new media. In fact, understanding these new platforms is not an option; it is a requirement. For instance, rather than fearing content generated in Web 2.0 forums, companies should use Web 2.0 tools to allow—and learn from—two-way communication with their customers.

When frustrated JetBlue customers launched a blog recounting the hours they were stranded on the tarmac during storms in February 2007, the New York City-based airline's CEO responded, not with a traditional press release, but by posting a video apology on YouTube. In its first week online, the video was viewed 40,000 times, and consumers sent JetBlue thousands of supportive e-mails and phone calls in response. In addition, pundits praised the airline for successfully incorporating social media into crisis communications.

Source: http://www.strategy-business.com/li/leadingideas/li00037?pg=1

Rapid development is key

Some Web applications require the services of professional developers and system integrators. Even as enterprises move toward a service-oriented architecture (SOA) model, where information from diverse systems is presented in a consistent Web interface, the ease and speed of integration projects depend on the degree to which the underlying applications adhere to open industry standards. Systems that are closed or proprietary are more complex—and therefore more costly—to integrate, and some vendors design their software in this way to maximize the revenue potential for their services organizations. The alternative is to go with software that is highly integrated out of the box and supported with a robust set of resources for professional developers, a global ecosystem of partners, and a widespread body of knowledge and skills. This approach not only simplifies the task of developing new e-business applications, but also provides businesses with a wider choice of partners and a more competitive market for IT services.

Self-service workflow automation

Real agility comes when professional IT resources are not required to design and deploy basic Web-based applications such as extranet portals, personalized Web sites, team workspaces, and task-based workflows for projects and documents. Self-service development puts the tools for business change in the hands of business users. These tools let them create customized e-business solutions within a framework where larger issues of security, access control, design guidelines, and content management still fall under the governance of IT.

Providing Flexible Solutions for Changing Business Needs

One of the key challenges of a dynamic business environment is providing the right tools in a rigid IT infrastructure that is typically found in today's enterprises. Most large businesses have implemented structured enterprise solutions to automate core business functions in finance, operations, supply chain management, and other critical areas—including compliance. These systems were probably designed around a specific set of workflows and requirements. When business needs change, the systems themselves must be updated, along with all of the dependencies that have grown up around them. People who change jobs need to be trained and retrained, rather than building one set of reusable software skills. In short, the rigidity and complexity of structured information systems can serve as dead weight on companies that need to move fast in changing times.

Flexible, proactive compliance

Regulatory compliance offers a concrete demonstration of the drawbacks of rigidity. In 2002, following the market contraction in the wake of the dot-com bust and 9/11, governments in the United States and Europe instituted new regulations on financial reporting. This triggered a $2.5 billion cycle of new IT investment in systems in 2002, with the reporting and security capabilities mandated by government—most with little additional business value beyond their compliance function.[8] According to a survey by Korn/Ferry International, the Sarbanes-Oxley Act, which imposed strict regulations on information reporting and internal controls on American businesses, Sarbanes-Oxley cost Fortune 500 companies an average of $5.1 million in compliance expenses in 2004.[9] As businesses explore expanding into new markets, the uncertainty surrounding regulation is magnified. The economy may be global, but governments are still local. Each will impose its own regulatory requirements, especially on businesses that appear to be operating in an opaque manner.

What is the solution to the quandary of coping with a dynamic business environment, given today's rigid IT environments? A flexible business solution architecture built on industry standards and designed to interoperate with the core IT platform simplifies compliance. First, it is easier to set and change policies and business rules around data retention, reporting, process consistency, and security as regulations change. More important, well-designed solution architectures enable companies to become proactively transparent, both internally and externally, in ways that may preempt the demand for government regulation in the first place.

TENETS FOR SUCCESS

The ability to manage a dynamic business is critical to the success of all organizations. Information technology is a strategic enabler of that success. However, not all IT strategies are created equal. Decisions about platforms, applications, and end-user environments matter—not just because they affect costs but because they can be decisive in providing the capabilities, flexibility, and agility needed by businesses to remain competitive in an uncertain world.

Software adds value by making it easier for businesses to rapidly adapt to new requirements and capitalize on new opportunities, especially in a global economy characterized by constant, unpredictable change and relentless competition. Most important, software allows an organization to effectively manage its competitive differentiators so that its unique value continues to attract customers. Customers seeking information technology solutions that increase the dynamic potential of their business should consider the following approaches:

Empower end users with tools that preserve IT governance. When business users have the ability to rapidly design, deploy, and manage solutions that adapt to new requirements, the business can react more quickly. In this environment, IT can spend more time and money on technology that enables competitive advantage and value-added governance, rather than on maintaining monolithic systems with architectures too constrained to adapt.

Reusable infrastructure creates reusable skills. Change always requires adjustment, but change anticipated by planning can smooth the transition. When business applications behave in familiar ways across functions, people can change roles and learn new skills more quickly, focusing on business knowledge rather than software knowledge. Likewise, when servers and applications in the data center share a common framework, a common development environment, and a common set of administrative tools, IT can manage more efficiently and build new capabilities on the existing platform more quickly.

Automate low-value tasks, enable high-value work. Structured applications provide efficiency by automating expansive workflow processes, but it is not cost-effective to custom-develop software to automate specific information tasks. Software must provide nontechnical business users with the ability to manage their own workflows, derive business insights from data, and support team activities. That way, they can benefit from process automation without incurring the costs associated with centralized information technology development and the specialized skills and support those types of systems require over time.

Business solutions should look and work like standard desktop applications. When core business solutions like enterprise resource planning (ERP), customer relationship management (CRM), and financial management applications are built on disconnected silos of data, business users become the point of integration. Often that means navigating multiple, inconsistent user interfaces, which reduces productivity and introduces errors. A consistent, familiar environment that brings enterprise data into standard information work applications that people already know and use makes business data more accessible and more useful.

Strategic information should be visible and accessible. In a dynamic business environment, decision makers need to be able to view their business and their market from commanding heights. Data from multiple systems within and beyond the enterprise should be exposed in common spaces (such as browsers and portals) and familiar applications (such as spreadsheets), in formats that simplify complex data into clear patterns for rapid analysis and action.

DYNAMIC BUSINESS: FORCES TO WATCH, UNCERTAINTIES TO CONSIDER

Force	What to Watch For
Globalization	What if there is a backlash to global economic integration, and outsourcing manufacturing to China or customer service to India suddenly becomes politically problematic or economically disadvantageous?
New Regulations	Recent systemic failures in regulating the financial markets, product safety, food purity, and other important areas seem to indicate that government will take a more assertive role in the future. But what if business offers more transparency, preempting the need for new regulations? Or what if consumers demand transparency nearly equal to formal regulation?
Disintermediation	E-business has virtually eliminated entire industries of brokers and middlemen (have you talked to a travel agent recently?). But consumers may also rediscover the value of accountable, empowered, and independent agents to simplify the increasingly unmanageable array of complexities and choices in the market.
Mobility	Mobile devices add convenience and raise expectations. How will innovation in devices and services continue to transform work and business?
New Markets	Growth continues in emerging markets, and the developed world is watching the BRIC (Brazil, Russia, India, China) bloc closely. But undiscovered pockets of potential remain in niche markets of established economies.

Force	What to Watch For
Climate Change	How rapidly will climate change make itself felt, and how will it redistribute geopolitical power? What opportunities will this create for new businesses and new public-private partnerships?
New Competitors	Where will competition come from? Established players who reinvent themselves in unexpected ways? Insurgents who suddenly rise out of nowhere? Encroachment from previously unrelated markets and industry? All of the above?
New Partnerships	What is your core business, and what can be handled at comparative advantage by establishing trading partnerships? How will these partnerships be organized and governed? How will partners share information, and how will trust be formed?
New Business Models	Open innovation, crowd-sourcing, on-demand media, viral marketing, the "Long Tail," and dozens of other new business models emerge constantly, challenging organizations and professionals to keep up. Which ones are fleeting, and which demand your attention? How can you spot them and react fast?
New Customer Expectations	With YouTube, everyone is a producer. With blogs, everyone is a pundit. With e-commerce, everything is just a click away. Does your customer experience empower people to this extent, or do old processes slow them down and frustrate them?
Security Concerns	Since the dawn of the Internet age, viruses and other malware threats have evolved along with systems and applications. Now, social engineering attacks exploit human weakness to get around high-tech security. What steps are necessary to stay ahead of the bad guys?
Disruptive Technology	What is the next game-changer? Robotics? Nanotechnology? How can organizations plan for the unexpected without getting caught leaning too far one way or the other?

Force	What to Watch For
Natural Disasters	The past few years have seen natural disasters, epidemics, and other catastrophes cost hundreds of thousands of lives and trillions of dollars. How durable are human-based networks and markets compared to the forces of nature?
Commodity Prices	Global economic growth is spiking demand for commodities, including food, oil, and raw materials, and driving prices through the roof. Will this volatility continue? Who wins, who loses, and how well positioned is your business to absorb the turbulence?
Environment and Natural Resources	Widespread growth also has environmental costs, especially in fast-growing emerging markets where governments lack the inclination or power to regulate. At the same time, consumer awareness of environmental issues is growing. What response will markets and governments develop to address the problems of environmental degradation and resource depletion?
Political Unrest	Demographics, economic uncertainty, ancient ethnic rivalries, and geopolitical competition continue to fuel unrest, even in countries usually considered stable. Are social and political institutions strong enough to manage rapid change, or will conflict supplant compromise?

NOTES

1. World Internet Usage and Population Statistics, May 21, 2008. www.internetworldstats.com
2. Virki, Tarmo. "Putting Customers to Work, Nokia Takes on the Web." *Reuters*, March 18, 2008.
3. Two good discussions of this can be found in: Tapscott, Don and Williams, A., *Wikinomics: How Mass Collaboration Changes Everything*. New York, NY, Portfolio, 2006; and Shirky, Clay. *Here Comes Everybody: The Power of Organizing without Organizations*. New York, NY, Penguin, 2008.
4. Anderson, Chris. *The Long Tail: Why the Future of Business Is Selling Less of More*. New York, NY, Hyperion, 2006.
5. "Tata Motors says Ford Deal to Improve Balance Sheet." *Reuters*, March 27, 2008

6. McGregor, Jena. "Consumer Vigilantes." *BusinessWeek* Special Report, February 21, 2008. www.businessweek.com/magazine/content/08_09/b4073038437662.htm
7. Feldman, Susan. "The High Cost of Not Finding Information" (as reported in studies by IDC and organizations such as the Working Council of CIOs, AIIM, the Ford Motor Company, and Reuters). *KM World*, March 1, 2004.
8. Evans-Correia, Kate. "New Regulations Spur IT Spending, Headaches." *Search-CIO.com*, December 22, 2003.
9. Korn/Ferry International's 31st Annual Board of Directors Study. "Price of Regulatory Compliance Skyrockets." November 22, 2004.

CHAPTER 3

Prospering in a Blended World

The workplace of the second decade in the millennium will be a study in diversity. Older workers will encounter younger workers with workplace perspectives that are very different than the ones they shared in their youth. Globalization has blurred the edges of nation, culture, and language, assuring that both the physical and virtual workplaces will be diverse. Technology has challenged traditional boundaries between work and life by bringing communication into personal space and permitting friendships and personal pursuits to penetrate the enterprise. It has redefined the meaning of structure and chaos while challenging long-held beliefs in boundaries between personal and public property. Even the edges of corporations are blurring as mergers and acquisitions redefine industries, competitors, and the influence on models of public corporations and private equity. The confluence of forces shaping today's organizations will give rise to a *Blended World* that calls for distinctly new approaches to managing customer and partner relationships, the workforce, and the very way we define work.

While external economic and regulatory forces are driving organizations to be more dynamic, the blended world is transforming organizations from within. No enforceable mandates exist to govern which workers to hire or where workers must be located; no global regulation dictates the operating language of a company; no legislation defines the value individuals place on digital content; and no external force ordains which roles are outsourced and which stay in-house. The blended world is a world of choice: a world cocreated from the business strategy, the attitudes, workstyles, and composition of the workforce, and the markets the company serves.

The successful organization will find ways to leverage the contrasting strengths of diverse perspectives found in its workforce and among its customers. It will retain the flexibility and entrepreneurialism necessary to transform internal policies and practices in a way that will help the company attract and retain talent, maximize the value derived from investments in people and infrastructure, and embrace the fuzziness at the edges of convention that will drive innovation. Information technology will be an important element in making the blended workplace a functional environment that achieves strategic objectives.

DRIVING FORCES

The following characteristics define the blended workplace:

Blended workforce. Demographically, the postwar Baby Boom generation in North America, Western Europe, and Japan is slowly giving way to a new global Millennial generation with a different approach to work and technology. Organizationally, in many companies the examination of core competencies has led to the outsourcing of roles that would have been unthinkable in the past, thus leading to a workforce that is increasingly contingent, contracted, or part-time.

Blended workstyles. Remote access, mobile devices, virtual communities, and other technology-mediated environments are driving the decentralization of organizations and workplaces, and work/life balance is an increasingly important component of workforce expectations and job satisfaction. With the core workforce facing the prospect of simultaneously caring for aging parents and young children, while still trying to maintain time for personal relationships and pursuits, organizations that foster work/life balance will be attractive to workers.

Blended world. The blurring of borders makes possible the integration of new partners, new supply networks, and new acquisitions to reach global markets and tap the talent of a global workforce.

Blended Workforce

Aging workforce

From Tokyo to Amsterdam to Indianapolis, the huge cohort of postwar Baby Boomers (born 1946–1962) is hurtling toward retirement age (see Figure 3.1, Changing U.S. Workforce). The U.S. Department of Labor Statistics estimates that nearly 10 million skilled jobs in the United States could go unfilled by 2010[1] (see Figure 3.2, Skilled Labor Shortage). Some labor markets are already feeling the squeeze (see Figure 3.3, Global Talent Shortage). About 180,000 British nurses are due to retire over the next 10 years.[2] And by 2020, the U.S. Health Resources and Services Administration projects that America will face a shortage of more than 1 million nurses.[3] Half of America's scientists and engineers are 40 and older. In the 1960s, space exploration captured the imagination of young engineers; today, only 4 percent of workers at the U.S. Space Agency NASA are under 30.[4]

And the U.S. population is relatively young by European standards, with less than 13 percent age 65 and older, ranking America as the 38th oldest country. In Europe, there are four people of working age for every person over 65; by 2050, this ratio will have dropped to two workers per pensioner. Except for Japan, the world's 15 oldest countries are all

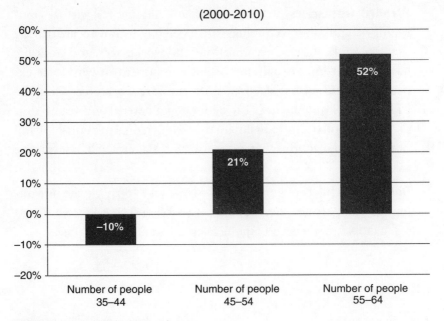

FIGURE 3.1   Changing U.S. Workforce

Source: U.S. Bureau of Labor Statistics

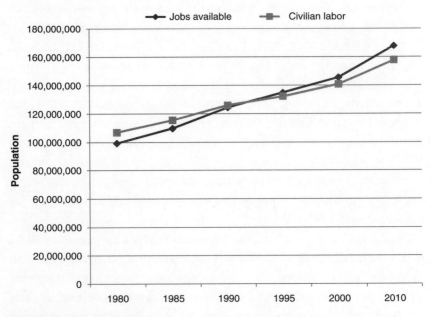

FIGURE 3.2   Skilled Labor Shortage

Source: Bureau of Labor Statistics, Department of Labor

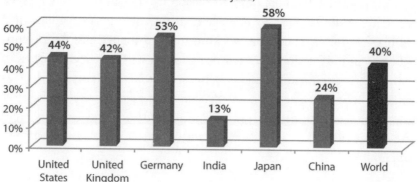

(% of responding employers indicating gap between available workers and available jobs)

FIGURE 3.3   Global Talent Shortage

Source: Manpower Inc.

in Europe. Japan is quickly becoming the world's oldest population. In a country with 66 million workers, one in four is 55 and older. In the United States that figure is one in six. By 2025, 27.3 percent, or 33.2 million, Japanese will be over 60.[5]

Middle management crunch

The next-youngest cohort to the Baby Boomers is much smaller worldwide. In the United States, the so-called "Generation X" or "GenXers" (born 1963–1980) numbers about 53 million compared to nearly 78 million Baby Boomers, and the falloff is even more dramatic in parts of Europe. As these workers approach midlife and mid-career, they are not as eager as their elders to work long hours at the expense of family time.

Bring on the Internet generation

Millennials (born 1981–2000) grew up with computers and the Internet. Their relationship with technology provides them with not only useful skills, but also a fundamentally networked view of organizations and a more informal approach to boundaries and relationships. Some employers already see challenges, as Millennials' notions run into the more hierarchical structures of traditional businesses.

Generation blend

The leverage of Millennials and, to a lesser extent, mid-career GenXers, is forcing some changes to management practices and organizational cultures. Employers are also working to keep their more senior contributors in the fold longer, attempting to forestall the inevitable loss of knowledge, relationships, and capabilities. As Rob Salkowitz discusses in his 2008 book, *Generation Blend: Managing Across the Technology Age Gap*, organizations must tread a careful path to blend the skills and knowledge of their veteran workers with the tech-enabled workstyle of Millennials.[6]

Rise of the contingent workforce

Contingent staff, outsourced employees, freelance workers, contractors, boutique service providers, or vendors: By any name you call them, these independent workers are changing the structure and expectations that governed the labor market through the Industrial Age. Today, there are more than 42 million independent workers in the United States, or 31 percent of the workforce. Their sheer numbers indicate a major shift in the expectations that have governed employment. In many organizations, the composition of the labor force is steadily shifting from full-time employees with benefits to arrangements with limits on benefits, time, mobility, and other factors. Many of those features fit well with the lifestyle choices of a flexible creative class, and with the employer's need for flexibility in its workforce. This trend will likely increase as Baby Boomers reach retirement age and seek alternative work arrangements.[7]

Twenty years ago, janitorial services were more commonly outsourced than any other services. Today, security, recruiting, design, information technology development and management, financial management, training, manufacturing, legal services, and many other functions are outsourced. In a meeting, it can be difficult to tell the difference between employees and contractors unless you look to subtle clues on identification badges. This growing workforce coexists and creates challenges around role definition, intellectual property protection, and business continuity. More diverse and more geographically distributed organizations will need to put strategies in place to manage the expectations and the results of these workers. With companies constantly examining their cost structure and fine-tuning their strategies, it is likely that the blend of employees, contingent staff, and contract workers will grow over the next decade.

The world has not seen such a dramatic shift in the characteristics of the workforce since the Industrial Age prompted young farmers to abandon their agrarian lives for urban and suburban futures. Companies will need to carefully consider how they will create a binding sense of organizational culture in light of disparate backgrounds and expectations and a wide range of work agreements.

Blended Workstyles

The blended world features a diversity of workstyles. Some people are uncomfortable with team members down the hall, let alone colleagues half a world away with a different language and different customs. Others thrive in an environment of teamwork and interpersonal challenges. Some people are uncomfortable withholding information from customers, no matter how proprietary it may be; others find any level of transparency a threat. Some are annoyed and distracted by interruptions; others who were raised on videogames, instant messaging, and the Web become bored with linear processes and repetitive assignments. Some people work best when they can create a productive work environment in their homes; others flourish best in an office. Some use standard-managed enterprise desktop PCs; others insist on integrating their own devices, software, and personal networks.

Smart organizations will find ways to manage across the varied expectations of today's workforce by supporting different work practices and technologies under the umbrella of sound management and IT governance. For example, Dow Corning uses various technologies to support a global collaborative culture (see The Formula for Collaboration).

The Formula for Collaboration

Dow Corning has had a collaborative culture for decades, so it is no surprise that the company has adopted various technologies to support its staff. Based in Midland, Michigan, Dow Corning has globally dispersed R&D teams that develop products based on silicon and silicone technologies, including sealants, adhesives, polymers, and many other materials.

Face time and telephones are still essential, but Web 2.0 tools are being used to make communication easier and to reduce travel. Dow Corning is also starting to make wide use of multipoint videoconferencing, Web conferencing, Internet telephony, and application sharing software. And the company has a document sharing system for its 10,000 workers.

Organizations need to clearly understand the blur between managed processes and specific processes, between structure and patterns governed by the need of the moment, and between highly governed infrastructure at the core of an organization, and the flexibility of putting the tools for change in the hands of those closest to the business.

Virtual workforce

The technology to enable remote and distributed work has been available for years, but management, human resources, and IT policy and practices have lagged behind. Many organizations unconsciously reinforce older practices by tying performance to time and place, or by discouraging the adoption of technology through the expectation of face-to-face meetings and rewards for physical availability.

In some organizations, expectations are adjusting to the technology, and the technology is improving as well. Workers of all ages seek greater work/life balance, and they can find it when given the choice of flexible hours and telecommuting. An employer's growing reliance on independent workers of all kinds reduces its need for physical space and increases the need for remote work. Communities and governments are also encouraging virtual workforces through telecommuting incentives and other policies that meet their obligations to manage the environmental, economic, and energy policy expectations of their constituencies.

In a world of choice, workers will bring their consumer behavior to their jobs. They will make more choices about where and when they work and, in stable economies, will either opt out of work situations that do not meet their personal needs, or negotiate more flexible time. Millennials can expect to have more than 20 jobs in seven to 10 careers over their working lives, and they have adjusted their expectations accordingly.[8] Employers are already experiencing loyalty and retention issues among younger workers. As Millennials gradually displace Baby Boomers, organizations will need to control workplace variables that lead to turnover. They will need to develop functional team practices, create opportunities for new workers to start on different aspects of the business quickly, and provide the latest technology and on-going learning even to the most junior team members.

Uniting the virtual workforce

Creating a successful virtual workforce requires adaptations by employers and the rest of the group: employees, contractors, contingent staff, consultants, and partners. Managers need to learn new practices and master new technologies to ensure that virtual teams perform as well as or better than collocated groups. IT must protect information shared by geographically distributed teams, including partners and other nonemployees, even beyond the firewall to satisfy business and regulatory requirements. Workers sometimes have to adjust their own ways of functioning and learn to collaborate more openly, bridging "virtual distance" through technology-mediated relationships. Global food company Nestlé USA Inc. relies on technology to facilitate cross-border communications (see Social Network for Cohesion).

Social Network for Cohesion

About two years ago, Nestlé USA Inc., the Glendale, California-based subsidiary of Nestlé S.A. of Vevey, Switzerland, launched a social network to encourage employees to meet and engage. The bigger goal was to help break down functional and location-based silos.

The social network, available only within the corporate firewall, is open to the more than 7,000 workers in several U.S. locations. Much like a public social networking site, users can post profiles, upload photos, and access content. More than 1,250 employees, including the CEO, have posted profiles.

All parties need to recognize that many factors lead to the success of a virtual team—from an acceptance of cultural differences to new ways of managing and measuring performance to new styles of communication. Organizations must not simply invest in information technology as a channel for communication and collaboration, but help teams develop processes that allow them to realize value through that investment.[9]

Attracting the global creative class

Thanks to networks and remote collaboration, knowledge workers no longer have to emigrate to sell their services to foreign employers. This dynamic is transforming the workforce from one that is mono-cultural and collocated to one that is multicultural and distributed. This transformation adds considerably to the complexity of management. Tacit knowledge, group dynamics, and shared cultural assumptions once helped bolster relationships within teams and across organizations. Now, practices and expectations must be made more explicit, and team dynamics must be managed with better awareness of potential differences among team members.

STRATEGIC WORKPLACE TECHNOLOGIES

Information technology can help people and organizations bridge the divides of age, workstyle, distance, and nationality. IT can also enable the blended workforce to add value through improved relationships with customers, partners, and talent pools to reduce costs by identifying new efficiencies and adding value through innovation in processes, products, and services. Information technology plays a role in the following three important areas:

1. **Knowledge management.** Enabling the retention and transfer of explicit and tacit knowledge across generations, cultures, and organizational boundaries.
2. **Mobility and virtual workforce management.** Extending the capabilities and protections of the enterprise and its data resources to people anywhere, anytime.
3. **Collaboration and coordination.** Reducing virtual distance, facilitating well-managed teamwork, and bringing partners into critical processes.

Knowledge Management

Knowledge management systems to capture and transfer human knowledge (as opposed to data records) gained a bad reputation in the 1990s because first-generation solutions focused more on technology than practice. In the blended workforce, knowledge management is not a fad but an essential strategy to ensure continuity of capabilities. Organizations cannot afford to lose the know-how of workers nearing retirement age, yet current efforts to keep senior staff in place with escalating salaries are unsustainable[10] (see Figure 3.4, The Challenge of Knowledge Capture and Sharing).

From knowledge systems to knowledge networks

A new generation of collaboration technology makes it easier to capture, expose, and consume knowledge without many of the drawbacks of earlier solutions. Blogs, wikis, RSS feeds, podcasts, and other rich media allow knowledge owners to share what they know in an accessible, informal style with the people who need it. Communities of practice are becoming more popular in fields such as healthcare and financial

Almost half of surveyed executives said knowledge capture and sharing is a significant challenge.

(% of respondents indicating the level of challenge on a scale of 1 to 5, with 1 being "not a challenge" and 5 being "a severe challenge")

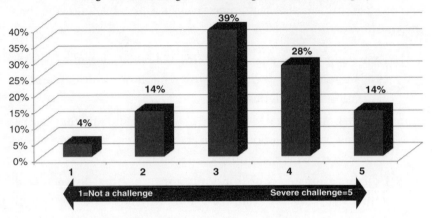

FIGURE 3.4   The Challenge of Knowledge Capture and Sharing

Source: The Accenture High Performance Workforce Study 2006 (http://www.accenture.com/Global/Consulting/Workforce_Performance/R_and_I/HighPerformaceStudy2006.htm)

services, creating networks of experts who can bring knowledge to bear on specific problems on short notice. One example is the Healthcare Financial Management Association (HFMA), an online forum for members to share knowledge in the healthcare finance industry.[11]

Another example of using blogging to enhance internal communications is at financial security company Northwestern Mutual (see, Blogging to Communicate).

Blogging to Communicate

For years, collaboration has been part of its culture, so it was natural for Northwestern Mutual to adopt internal blogging. CEO Ed Zore actively promoted the project, encouraging employees at the Milwaukee-based financial security company to communicate more widely across departments. He especially wanted to hear what was on his employees' minds.

That was nearly four years ago, and soon after, Northwestern Mutual launched MutualBlog on its intranet. To help kick things off, the company

recruited about 10 "seed" bloggers. Any worker can start a blog or participate in one, and between 500 and 1,000 employees are active users among
Northwestern Mutual's 5,500 employees. Many workers read the blogs but
do not post.

Blogs are now used widely for project collaboration and management. One
of the most popular blogs is written by a more senior employee who blogs
on how to get things done—all the unwritten rules newer workers do not
know. There is even a blog about how to blog properly.

Source: Bill Roberts, interview

Making knowledge easier to find and use

Once information is in the digital realm, improved enterprise search
engines and expertise location systems can make it easier for users to
find data and documents and to initiate relationships with the right
people if the documents and discussion archives are not enough. Social
networks, such as those offered by Facebook and LinkedIn, enable people
to create durable structures to support relationships, maintain contact,
keep one another up to date, and facilitate in-person meetings when
appropriate. Siemens is a great example of an organization relying on a
social networking site to enhance peoples' ability to find expertise within
a huge global organization (see Embracing Facebook—Sort Of).

Embracing Facebook—Sort Of

The workforce at Siemens, the engineering conglomerate headquartered in
Germany, could not be any more diverse—400,000 employees in dozens of
countries. In this global situation, it is not easy to create methods of informal
communication, but employees have found one solution that management
has accepted for the time being.

In mid-2007, managers in the United States noticed a growing number of
employees using Facebook to network with fellow workers. Only a fraction
of the total workforce—about 7,000—have profiles identifying themselves

(continued)

as Siemens workers, but for now Facebook serves as the company's unofficial social networking site.

Siemens does not know who started using Facebook first, and for reasons no one has figured out, the heaviest use is in Scandinavia, Turkey, and the Middle East. The company is now working on social media guidelines for appropriate use, just as it previously did for blogging, which many employees use inside the firewall.

Source: Bill Roberts, interview

Practices to support learning

These technologies alone cannot solve the knowledge problem, however. They must be supplemented with practices, training, acculturation, and possibly even changes to compensation models to encourage appropriate levels of participation. Organizations should be aware of generational, cultural, and role-based differences in trust and acceptance, in addition to hidden disincentives that can inhibit adoption.

A great example of applying technologies to enhance training is how Delaware North Companies uses the Web to train its managers (see Consistent Training on the Web).

Consistent Training on the Web

In the past two years, Delaware North Companies Inc. (DNC), a hospitality and food services provider based in Buffalo, New York, with 40,000 employees globally, has delivered management training over the Internet for its 3,000 managers.

When DNC used to rely on local executives and HR managers to train new supervisors, the results varied widely. To address this problem, the Web-based program has four levels aimed at all managers—from frontline supervisors to executives. Each level includes self-paced interactive modules that the manager completes online, with follow-up meetings in a virtual classroom via a conference call.

In the virtual classes, the teacher uses Web tools, including an electronic white board and polling to involve participants. The executive level of training is a blend of the Web-based effort and projects and other activities in an actual classroom. The training is not only cost effective but also has reach, consistency, and much of the richness of traditional classroom-based training. Nearly 200 managers have completed at least one level of training.

Source: Bill Roberts, interview.

One promising approach is to pair social computing technology with traditional mentoring programs, bringing knowledgeable but possibly reticent older workers together with their inexperienced, tech-savvy colleagues to share information in a reciprocal way. Younger workers not only gain insights from the mentor and form relationships that connect them more closely to the workplace culture, but they can also ease the training and support burden on IT by imparting technology tips in a comfortable, discrete setting. This practice will prove most effective when both parties include learning as part of their commitments, with knowledge transfer registered as a measurable outcome at review time.

Mobility and Virtual Workforce Management

The virtual workforce is enabled by pervasive high-speed wired and wireless networks, powerful mobile computing devices, and content-level security to protect data in transmission or on a lost device. In addition, software that provides unified communications services across voice, e-mail, fax, instant messaging, videoconferencing, application sharing, and shared calendar applications helps keep mobile and remote workers closely connected to colleagues across the office or around the world.

Reducing virtual distance

Innovations in real-time communication software and technology, particularly in videoconferencing, continue to improve the experience of online meetings. Next-generation Web cameras triangulate speakers in a conference room, and new room-based systems use sophisticated algorithms to track speakers and automatically switch focus to the current speaker. Larger monitors and high-bandwidth signals offer better resolution images and sound. Corporations such as Procter & Gamble, Wachovia, PepsiCo, and AIG are investing in large-scale telepresence technology, which could become more mainstream within the next several years.[12] Technology will need to be combined with new practices, as Karen Sobel Lojeski and Richard R. Reilly point out in their book *Uniting the Virtual Workforce*; and organizations will need to embrace new ways of working across space and time.[13]

Managing the blended workforce

Smarter software is helping remote workers be more productive and giving managers some visibility into their work habits when close supervision is required. Presence technology, usually indicated by the colored "pawn" icons in instant messaging applications to show whether a person is available, away, or busy enables people to manage their exposure to real-time communications, such as phone calls, instant messages, and text messages, while making their work status visible to managers and colleagues. For organizations that are hesitant about potential productivity issues with workers who are not physically present, application-specific presence can tell managers what remote people are working on, what documents they have open, how many keystrokes or mouseclicks have occurred in the past few minutes, and other productivity metrics. However, some organizations find that productivity increases when they trust workers and measure on outcomes rather than track processes.

Protecting content beyond the firewall

Content-based security using information rights management (IRM) technology and server-based encryption can protect documents, passwords, and devices from unauthorized access, even beyond the firewall. Current IRM enables system administrators to set access policies on entire documents. As this technology matures, it will be possible to push down policies to elements within documents, such as formulas in a spreadsheet, listings in an address book, lines of text, or slides in a presentation, with the document automatically redacting itself based on the access permissions of the user.

Collaboration and Coordination

Collaboration and coordination software unites the blended workforce and makes the experience of working together as natural and productive as working in the same physical location. Now more powerful, integrated applications and services for social computing, including RSS feeds, wikis, blogs and social networks, are joining the arsenal of collaboration tools available to businesses, as they become more secure and manageable in the enterprise. Use of these tools is growing (see Figure 3.5, Web 2.0 Use).[14] Facilities such as project workspaces, document repositories, team access to contact and schedule information, shared project flowcharts, shared task lists, and automated notifications provide a foundation for virtual teamwork by keeping everyone's status and work visible. Team members can see shared information in the periphery of their standard work environment, or they can access up-to-the-minute data from any portable device.

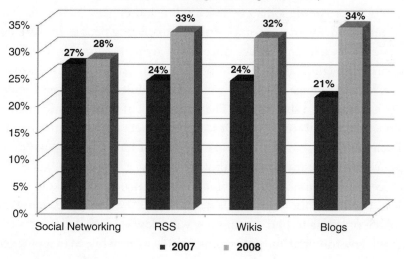

Based on a June, 2008 survey of 1,988 executives worldwide and a January, 2007 survey of 2,847 executives worldwide, use of Web 2.0 apps is increasing.
(% of companies using technologies or tools)

FIGURE 3.5 Web 2.0 Use

Source: McKinsey (http://www.mckinseyquarterly.com/Building_the_Web_20_Enterprise_McKinsey_Global_Survey_2174_abstract)

Supporting diverse workstyles

A standard collaboration environment is well-suited for the uncertainties of a dynamic, diverse workforce, because it can support a wide range of workplace scenarios—from intramural project teams to cross-industry communities of practice to extranets that extend access to partners and independent providers worldwide to rapid response teams charged with business continuity through a crisis. If the collaboration services are standard, consistent across roles and applications, and well-integrated with familiar information work tools, people will only need to adopt one set of work practices and learn one set of software skills to participate fully in a distributed, collaborative environment. Consistency and simplicity can reduce training requirements for less sophisticated or change-averse members of the workforce while supporting the desires of all workers to acquire skills that will be broadly useful in a long, diverse, and unpredictable career.

Simplifying management complexity

For managers, project coordination and process design tools can make it easier to create, track, and manage complex workflows for distributed teams. By automating low-value tasks, such as updates and notifications, and providing a map of tasks, roles, and dependencies, software can remove many of the complexities of managing people who are not physically present and reduce uncertainty by making processes visible. Instant messaging, as part of unified communications, can help managers take advantage of gaps in workers' schedules to offer coaching or to collaborate on a shared task. The integration of presence information into e-mail clients, mail messages, and elsewhere provides opportunity directly in the document, so workers will not have to shift to another application to see the status of another worker.

Technology, combined with practice and patience, will make communication and collaboration more fluid. And as the edges between work and life continue to blur, technology will allow workers to take control of their environment and deliver on commitments while managing their own time and personal relationships in the space where they are most comfortable or most productive—or simply where they happen to be at the moment.

BLENDING BEYOND THE WORKPLACE

Although the blended world most profoundly impacts the workplace, it reaches beyond the traditional sphere of employment. Organizations must recognize that the way their products are perceived is also blurring, as entire groups of consumers shift their value considerations based on new economics, new social priorities, and new technologies. Environmental consciousness is driving "green consumerism," with growing numbers of customers paying closer attention to the source, packaging, and environmental impact of the products they buy.

The music industry, for example, has encountered the challenge of changing business models as the Internet and unprotected digital media formats have sapped revenues from physical media such as CDs and DVDs.[15] This blurring of free and paid business models was the subject of a *Wired* magazine cover story, "Free! Why $0.00 is the Future of Business,"[16,17] that details a number of reasons why technology investments in the Web, and the spreading of those investments across millions of users, eventually drives the entry cost for businesses to zero. The physical assets of sales, once the focus of attention, have become marketing material—in the case of CDs, it is material for concerts, t-shirts, and posters. Writer Matt Mason describes the business potential of blending free and paid, licit and "pirate" distribution models in his book *The Pirate's Dilemma*.[18]

But the free/paid model is only one of the blends that businesses need to watch. The idea of structure is also open to reinterpretation. Previously unstructured data is gaining structure through metadata—descriptive fields that give context to the information and facilitate search and organization. This change is creating new opportunities to link data from traditional databases with free-form content such as rich media or handwritten notes, and providing new, more meaningful insights where fact and opinion, conjecture, and truth can coexist to provide all of the perspectives on a business issue that might once have been seen as black and white.

For centuries, we thought we understood the concept of "proprietary," but that too is now subject to redefinition and boundaries blur and barriers collapse. Companies are opening up their systems and their processes so that they can become platforms for technology or commerce, using their mastery of the standard and their service models to stave off competitors that may be equally compliant but less agile or innovative in how the standard is applied.

The concept of "open systems" has gained traction as the costs of mass collaboration have collapsed, leading to innovative new approaches to a variety of core activities that previously took place within the four walls of the company.[19] Everything from customer support to marketing to software development is now open to community participation, with varying levels of success and risk depending on the implementation and the customer base. Moving forward, the boundaries between open and proprietary will continue to blur, creating space for companies to experiment in the concept of cocreation with partners, customers, and large anonymous communities, while continuing to provide the single point of accountability that customers require.

Mergers and acquisitions create a blurring of companies that can be confusing to customers looking for a single point of contact or a consolidated view. This blurring also requires organizations to quickly find the intersections between business processes and finances to meet regulatory requirements and requirements generated by the merger itself. Between 65 percent and 80 percent of M&As destroy shareholder value rather than enhance it, according to Harvard Business School's Stephen Kaufman.[20] Overpriced bids that incur debt are a big cause of failure. But another cause is the complexity of integration, which often undermines the best intended goals, according to Dan Dalton, a professor at Indiana University's Kelley School of Business.[21]

The blended economy is not merely resulting in hybrid companies, but hybrid industries, as consumer expectations evolve in tandem with product innovation. The boundaries between content creation and content delivery have been blending for some time (McLuhan coined the phrase "the medium is the message" in the 1960s, after all). Auto manufacturers increasingly recognize themselves as being in the entertainment industry rather than just manufacturing. Hospitality firms deliver an experience, not just a hotel room. Businesses must stay vigilant to these kinds of perceptual changes, which will only accelerate as blend becomes the norm and firm boundaries the exception.

And in the financial world, growth and sustainability are blurring in the form of triple bottom-line reporting[22] that captures not only an organization's financial health but its ecological and social impacts. The argument is that, for publicly reported companies, this type of reporting provides a more holistic view to regulatory agencies, shareholders, and consumers. Given the lack of standards for social and ecological reporting, the new bottom lines are more about perception than reality, at least until standard forms of measurement emerge.

These and many other factors are reshaping the business world of the 21st Century. There is no single approach to navigating these changes, but information technology will play an important role in connecting the right people to the right information. It will bring together the sources of information that make up customer records and create a single view to assist both them and the agents with whom they speak. Information technology will also create new insights as it finds patterns between structured and unstructured data, and it will be the key to disintermediation as the new economics of the knowledge economy manifest themselves in customer desires and consumer constraints.

In the most successful organizations, information technology will be supplemented by anticipatory management, flexible strategy, and open and honest communication between consumers and companies and among workers and those who employ them. Perhaps most important, information technology will help organizations manage the complexity of the blurring, understand the answer in a given situation, and leap to action once that answer becomes clear.

TENETS FOR SUCCESS

The ability to execute strategy and manage expectations in a blended world is crucial to the success of all organizations. Information technology is a strategic enabler of that success. However, not all information technology strategies are created equal. Decisions about platforms, applications, and end-user environments matter, not just because these pieces affect costs but because they can be decisive in providing the capabilities, speed, and choices businesses need to compete in an uncertain world.

Software adds value by simplifying complexity and reducing the burden on managers and workers. Customers seeking effective information technology solutions that increase the performance and flexibility of the blended workplace should look for the following:

Familiar end-user environment. Knowledge sharing and collaboration depend on user participation. When end users have to learn new skills and practices to do their jobs, it increases the friction associated with any new deployment and can inhibit adoption. Collaboration capabilities embedded in the familiar environment of standard work applications are easier to learn and use, require less support, and provide transferable skills for workers and flexibility for employers.

Consistent experience across devices and modes of collaboration. People connect to their information through various devices and applications, more so now in the increasingly virtual workplace. Providing a consistent presentation of information and capabilities for workers, whether they use a PC, a mobile device, or a browser, helps reduce the cognitive barriers that create "virtual distance" while simplifying the amount of synchronization necessary to support a mobile workstyle.

End-user customization, IT standardization. The management challenge in a blended world is to accommodate multiple workstyles while maintaining information governance. A proliferation of end-user tools increases administration and support costs, complexity, and risk. But a one-size-fits-all model restricts workers' ability to add value, and it can prove unappealing to younger workers. The solution is a centrally managed platform where IT sets global policies for access, security, and data retention while workers have wide latitude to design and deploy custom solutions for their own business scenarios and personal workstyles using tools designed for nontechnical users.

Get out in front. Foresight is critical in a blended world. If you look ahead and guess wrong, you may be at risk, but if you do not look ahead at all, you will certainly be at risk. High-level discussions of business value and restrictive IT policies cannot keep Web 2.0 tools out of your enterprise if people want to use them. Recognize the factors that are driving potentially insecure consumer technologies into the enterprise—demand for fast, simple ways to connect with people and information—and look for enterprise-grade solutions that deliver these capabilities in a secure, centrally managed framework.

Global support. In a world blended across national borders, enterprise infrastructure requires an international network of developers, application providers, and integrators. This base of information technology partners must have knowledge and competency that extends deep into local markets around the world and is anchored by a provider with world-class abilities and global reach.

No matter what kind of economic models evolve, no matter whom a company hires or where it decides to do business, no matter how virtual or localized, the principles previously outlined are crucial, because it is an organization's *people* who will need to navigate the changes that confront them. The more an organization can do to empower its people—with practice, with policy, and with technology—the more adaptive it will be. The constraints of old models are impediments to innovation in today's economy. The more organizations resist the changes suggested by their younger workers and their new customers, the more disconnected they will be from their markets. And their risk of becoming less relevant as the market expectations shift will increase. Software is the only cost-effective tool for integrating flexible, fluid, organic models of management with solid foundations that support and map the organization's underlying governance models and data security needs. The blended world is calling for new architectures for business infrastructure as much as it is new structures for policy and practice. As those two needs co-evolve, the organizations that thrive will prove more resilient and more robust in the face of change, because they were forged by change and recognize it not as a threat, but as a source of innovation.

BLEND TRENDS

Here is a summary of the areas where blending will affect business over the next decade.

Trend	Overview
Work/Life Balance	The boundary between work and life will continue to blur, and the punctuated workday will become a standard in most occupations. This change will create opportunities for more job sharing and increase demand for technology that allows workers to engage with family and friends without being disconnected from the workplace.
Consumer Technology in Business	Just as the PC and instant messaging brought new capabilities to the workplace, so too will many emergent Web technologies. Consumer technology will impact business in many ways. Among them: building corporate brand on video sites; acquiring temporary virtual workforces through social networking to tackle specific problems; educating through mobile devices; and discovering relationships and patterns by combining data sets that drive innovation.
Making the Personal Public	From random thoughts in blogs to milestone life events, people are making their personal lives increasingly public. The Internet has created a vast repository of the personal in a public setting. Most platforms support some level of user control and security, but an increasingly unworried public is not turning them on, and older users may not fully embrace the culture of participation due to lingering fears about privacy.
Freelance Planet	The workforce will become more loosely coupled as organizations move tasks beyond the four walls and increase the blend between full-time employees and freelance workers. Unlike the work performed in the collaborative enterprise, these freelance workers may have short-duration jobs and not be as attached to processes or execution as those associated with outsourced functions.

Trend	Overview
The Collaborative Enterprise	As organizations outsource more, the reliance on internal process excellence will move to process intersections—with emphasis on handoffs and coordination costs between partners.
Baby Boom Becomes Millennial	With increased life expectancies, Baby Boomers may opt for early retirement or just leaving a company to prepare for their next career—one in which they may choose to work fewer hours. With the already apparent high turnover of the Millennial generation, organizations will face a constant churn of human capital and challenges with business continuity.
Communal Intellectual Property	Many things once considered valuable because of their physical presence will become more communal as their information components are extracted. Although intellectual property protection (IP) and licensing will continue, business models will emerge that take advantage of communal IP.
Transparent Organizations	Information that was once closely held will be made public, voluntarily or otherwise, so that stakeholders and other constituencies—including customers—understand what they are consuming and with whom they have relationships. The Institute of the Future sees this as one aspect of reciprocal accountability.
Corporate Culture	As mergers and acquisitions continue at increasing (but variable) rates, companies will have to place an emphasis on the blending of corporate cultures. This blending will include not just process and practice but a clear recognition and respect for the local cultural differences of workers, partners, and contractors.
Corporate Language	Organizations will continue to choose a language for their business, but many will face the need to create a semantic layer that will bind their corporation together. Many companies have internal acronyms that define their corporate-speak. And the blurring of boundaries may accelerate this trend, to the point that institutional argots evolve into living linguistic constructs.

Trend	Overview
Home Work and Placeless Work	Rising gas prices and the need for work/life balance create a demand for home-based offices that complement or replace corporate offices. Many organizations will begin to downsize their real estate holdings and opt out of lease renewals as the Internet and related technologies blur the edges of the physical corporation. With mobile technology, people will also choose to be placeless, their user ID and presence information substituting for a cubical location.
Customers as Employees	Customers will start acting like employees, self-servicing their needs (the way they print airline boarding passes). They will provide collaborative product input and support to other customers.
Shared Data	Consumers will create relationships, rules of engagement, and service-level agreements that govern how, when, and what parts of personal data—be it healthcare records, employment history, tax records, or credit history—are updated and accessed. For example, healthcare records will be owned by patients, but many parties will have some responsibility for their security or accuracy.
Integration of Space and Earth	Increased use of satellite imagery, global positioning systems, and other location data originating from space will increasingly blend with Earthbound sensors and commerce. Current use of such imagery and data to help plan disaster relief and military campaigns hint at the potential future opportunities for real estate developers, retailers, and other sectors to use these technologies. Commerce may even emerge from the shackles of gravity with space tourism and space-station–based research. Consumers, the public and private sectors, and the military will need to collaborate on policies governing earth orbit and beyond.

NOTES

1. U.S. Bureau of Labor Statistics, 2004 estimate.
2. Rose, David. "Nurses Leave for Australia in Thousands as NHS Halts Recruitment." *TIMESONLINE*, February 17, 2007.

3. Kuehn, Bridget M. "Global Shortage of Health Workers, Brain Drain Stress Developing Countries." *JAMA*, 2007.
4. Wolfe, Ira S. "Labor Storm Watch. The Perfect Labor Storm is About to Sweep Over Us." *Business 2 Business*, February 2006.
5. Sparrow, William. "When Freaky-Deaky Equals Hara-Kiri." *Asian Times*, March 8, 2008. http://www.atimes.com/atimes/Japan/JC08Dh01.html
6. Salkowitz, R. *Generation Blend: Managing Across the Technology Age Gap.* Hoboken, NJ: Wiley & Sons, 2008. This book is part of the Microsoft Executive Leadership Series.
7. Freelancers Union. "Defining the Independent Workforce: What is It, Why is It Expanding, and What are its Challenges?" Independent Workforce Issue Brief. http://www.freelancersunion.org/advocacy/issue-briefs/what-is-the-independent-workforce.pdf
8. Salkowitz, R. *Generation Blend: Managing Across the Technology Age Gap.* Hoboken, NJ: Wiley & Sons, 2008.
9. For a fuller discussion of virtual distance and management practices, see: Sobel Lojeski, Karen and Reilly, R. R. *Uniting the Virtual Workforce: Transforming Leadership and Innovation.* Hoboken, NJ: Wiley & Sons, 2008. This book is part of the Microsoft Executive Leadership Series.
10. Coy, Peter. "Golden Paychecks." *BusinessWeek*, July 2, 2007. http://www.businessweek.com/magazine/content/07_27/c4041003.htm?chan = search
11. Healthcare Financial Management Association. www.hfma.org
12. Wolgemuth, Liz. "'Telepresence' Enhances Video Conferencing. Cisco, HP, and Others Offer State-of-the-Art, High-Definition Systems." *U.S. News & World Report*, February 28, 2008.
13. Sobel Lojeski, Karen and Reilly, R. R. *Uniting the Virtual Workforce.* Hoboken, NJ: Wiley & Sons, 2008.
14. McKinsey. "Building the Web 2.0 Enterprise: McKinsey Global Survey." July 2008. http://www.mckinseyquarterly.com/Building_the_Web_20_Enterprise_McKinsey_Global_Survey_2174_abstract
15. Hiat, Brian and Serpick, E. "The Record Industries Decline." *Rolling Stone Rock and Roll Daily* Blog, posted June 28, 2007.
16. Anderson, Chris. "Free! Why $0.00 is the Future of Business." *Wired*, March 2008. http://www.wired.com/techbiz/it/magazine/16–03/ff_free?currentPage = 2
17. *Ibid.*
18. Mason, Matt. *The Pirate's Dilemma: How Youth Culture is Reinventing Capitalism.* New York, NY, Free Press, 2008.
19. See Shirkey, Clay. *Here Comes Everybody: The Power of Organizing without Organizations.* New York, NY: Penguin, 2008, for one of several recent takes on this subject.
20. Worthen, Ben. "How Coty Tackled Post-Merge Supply Chain Integration." CIO.com, January 15, 2007.
21. *Ibid.*
22. Wikipedia. "Triple Bottom Line." http://en.wikipedia.org/wiki/Triple_bottom_line

CHAPTER 4

Insights from Complexity

The world is being flooded by new data. Mobile devices and digital instruments are bringing information from the physical world into the digital realm. The most granular processes and transactions of business are now captured in powerful enterprise systems. Content on the Internet is increasing in magnitude. Collaboration data, from e-mail, instant messaging, community sites, blogs, and dozens of other sources crowds the margins of the information space with commentary, insight, and context. The insights we gain from analyzing this complex data are transforming everything from business to our fundamental understanding of nature and the universe (see Complexity in the Natural Sciences).

This wealth of new information has produced an embarrassment of riches for organizations that face the competitive requirement to take action based on the things they see happening in the world. When the view of the world is simple, strategies are clear. As the picture gets crowded with bits and bytes all screaming their significance, information can transform from a benefit to a burden. The explosion of new data—and the requirement to make sense of it—is driving the next level of innovation in software: deriving insight from complexity. No longer is it sufficient to make data available, or to create dashboards that reveal the complexities of a business. Today's executives, managers, and other business professionals demand new ways to turn information into action. They adopt key performance indicators (KPIs) as a process that sifts through data, allowing them to focus on the most important information. Sometimes, the most important information does not come from a single source. It is an index of sources that exposes a function's health along multiple, interrelated dimensions. And in some cases, even KPIs fail to capture true causal effects, because not all of the data required to understand the business is owned by the business. Today's organization is feeling pressure to open its perspective and find new ways to gain insight from this complexity. Tomorrow, the insights driven by data may mean the difference between a strong competitive position and survival. Gaining insights from complexity will no longer be a luxury; it will be a necessity.

Complexity in the Natural Sciences

The natural world is full of complexities, from the macro level of cosmology down to the quantum level of subatomic particles—from the evolutionary history of life to the behavior of the internal structures within cells—from the role of communication in society to the role of RNA in communication within cells. In turn, new data generates new classes of questions. Breakthrough tools in astronomy reveal the cosmos in stunning detail, revealing relationships between forces and body that push astronomers and physicists to reconsider what was once the common assumption. As new technologies and new instruments allow us to observe natural phenomena more closely, the picture that emerges is one of increasing uncertainty rather than clarity, of interconnectedness and surprise rather than the determinism of particles moving in a vacuum. In the same way, tools in business are expanding the view of managers and workers by giving them access to information and releasing them from the historical isolation of their functions. Organizations are complex systems. The more they interact, the more possibilities emerge from the interaction. And the closer we observe them, the richer these patterns appear.

DRIVING FORCES

Several forces today drive the increasing complexity of business:

- **Proliferating data.** Data is flooding into organizations from new sources—along with expectations that businesses can and should use that information to optimize processes, support higher levels of regulatory compliance, and serve customers better. Can organizations learn to *master the growing volume of data*?

- **Data as a strategic, competitive weapon.** If you can ask the right questions of your data, you can discover hidden relationships and points of leverage that can revolutionize business performance. The question is, can you find them before your competition does, and *turn your insights into a competitive advantage*?

- **Collaborative work.** As work becomes more collaborative, it also becomes more complicated. People must learn to navigate through a dense thicket of information, relationships, and processes. How can we make things simpler for them and empower people to *work effectively in a collaborative environment*?

Master the Growing Volume of Data

Emerging sources of data

Information is increasing at an exponential rate, and it can be divided into several categories:

- *Emerging.* Technologies such as radio-frequency identification (RFID), global positioning systems (GPS), digital instruments, vehicle-based telematics systems, and surveillance equipment create enormous volumes of new information that managers can use to measure performance and drive decision making.

- *Legacy data.* Legacy data from standalone systems, mainframes, and paper records is becoming more visible across the business as it is integrated into data warehouses.
- *Mobile sources.* Media-equipped mobile devices, such as smartphones, digital cameras, and portable gaming equipment create entirely new channels. Camera phones feed a growing body of rich-media content that consumes storage resources and is more difficult to tag and track than structured data.
- *Collaboration.* E-mail, instant messaging, workspaces, wikis, blogs, social networks, Web content management, and document repositories produce large amounts of unstructured data. These sources also produce metadata that reports on the state of content, its categories, and the relationships between data stored in thousands of locations. Over time, as better tools allow people to search data quickly and accurately, the way they view content will completely change.

Organizations are increasingly challenged to use this data—by itself and in combination with other internal and external sources—to improve processes and internal controls throughout the business. Collecting the data is no longer enough. People in all roles need access to the information and the tools for analysis that can help them bring insights to bear on their areas of responsibility.

Finding insights hidden in your data

An organization's own data about customers or processes is usually the first—and occasionally the best—place to start looking for insights that can improve business performance. Business intelligence techniques can be applied to any kind of data stored in a database and, very often, to other data, such as e-mails, memos, and presentations. It is common today for an organization to examine its customer records in new and unique ways to discover which products are most profitable, which customers are most valuable, or what new products, processes, or services can be introduced. In some industries—for example, insurance—the insight may lead to not taking a customer, because of the risk that the customer's past behavior predicts.

People armed with enough information and the right tools can accurately forecast market conditions with confidence. For example, the Web site FareCast, recently acquired by Microsoft Corporation, has developed a method for analyzing potential changes in ticket prices on specific air routes, so it sells insurance to offset the risk of overpaying. FareCast uses mostly public data in its calculations; the company's value derives from the relationships that human experts see within the data to provide unique insights and services to air travelers.[1]

There are many examples of how unexpected insights can be gleaned from data, such as Exelon Corp.—one of the world's largest utilities—using meter reading information to reduce power outages (see Exelon: More Power from Existing Data). These benefits can also extend to areas outside of business. For instance, researchers at the Institute of Crime Science, University College London, have found through computer simulations that burglaries actually spread very much like contagious diseases. The research reveals that crime is the result of human behavior combined with the physical spaces in which criminals find themselves, and not as much about the psychological makeup of the criminal. Crime, in some ways then, is a normal outcome of social interactions and the way societies evolve.[2] Insights like this are just waiting to be plucked from databases.

Exelon: More Power from Existing Data

As one of America's largest electric utilities, Exelon Corp. understands the power and unexpected insights that can come from existing data. The utility, with headquarters in Chicago, keeps tabs on 1.7 million electric meters and 500,000 gas meters in Philadelphia with an automated meter reading (AMR) system that transmits use and security information wirelessly every five minutes. Wanting even more value from its data, Exelon launched a pilot program to compare meter readings to actual events, and to predict

(continued)

impending power failures. As a result, crews will be able to prevent problems without going into disruptive "emergency mode."

"Utilities normally don't associate AMR information with reducing operational outages," says Glen Pritchard, a consulting engineer at Exelon. "We're finding more innovative ways to draw value from the AMR information. All of this helps reduce the chance or duration of an outage, which greatly enhances customer satisfaction."

Looking beyond traditional metrics

Some organizations are now reexamining their business models as senior executives realize that data from their operations and customers can be a source of new revenue. Beyond that, insight will come from data and information across the company's holdings and from its interactions with customers and suppliers (see Figure 4.1, BI Spreading Throughout Organizations). Strategic implications come from looking past the traditional KPIs, operational performance metrics, financial measures, and reporting requirements.

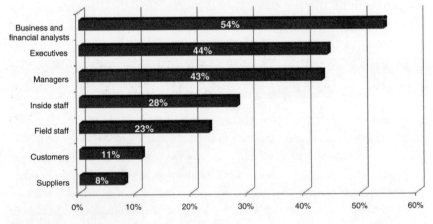

Business intelligence applications are moving beyond analysts and top executives to even suppliers and customers.

(% of companies reporting access provided to specific roles)

Role	%
Business and financial analysts	54%
Executives	44%
Managers	43%
Inside staff	28%
Field staff	23%
Customers	11%
Suppliers	8%

FIGURE 4.1   BI Spreading Throughout Organizations

Source: Howson, Cindy. *Successful Business Intelligence: Secrets to Making BI a Killer App.* New York, NY: The McGraw-Hill Companies, 2008

Applying data-based insights in qualitative ways

Distributed computing, which harnesses the unused processing power of networks of desktop PCs and devices along with data center assets, provides the raw horsepower for industrial-strength number-crunching without the costs of ownership. Moving forward, this means that data-based decision making is no longer dependent on the ability to afford overwhelming IT assets; anyone with the talent to ask the right questions can have access to the insights gleaned from quantitative analysis.

Turn Insights into Competitive Advantage

Organizations can take advantage of the wealth of data available to see opportunities that competitors miss. Cost and effectiveness are always important drivers of business performance, but understanding where costs are located or which processes are least efficient is difficult without deeply understanding their structures. The penetration of IT systems into the deepest reaches of the business, with the immediate purpose of driving particular efficiencies through automation, is also producing a flood of highly detailed operational data as a byproduct (see Figure 4.2, Operational BI Fuels Efficiency and Productivity).

Organizations can gain insights by looking at how this data alters over time in response to different inputs and changes to external conditions—even if those inputs and conditions do not seem at first to have a causal relationship to operations. By discovering these hidden cause-and-effect relationships, decision makers can quickly implement

Companies ranked the top benefits of operational business intelligence in the following order:

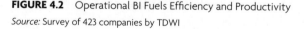

1. Improves operational efficiency
2. Enables workers to be more proactive
3. Provides better customer service
4. Catches problems before they escalate
5. Increases business transparency

FIGURE 4.2   Operational BI Fuels Efficiency and Productivity

Source: Survey of 423 companies by TDWI

The top six strategic applications of customer information by marketers include the following:

- Up-selling and cross-selling
- Segmenting and targeting
- Driving retention, loyalty, and promotional programs
- Identifying new opportunities and unmet needs
- Improving customer service
- Shaping personalized and customized communications

FIGURE 4.3   How Companies Use Customer Information

Source: Survey by the Chief Marketing Officer (CMO) Council

new strategies that may seem counterintuitive but actually result in improved performance and increased efficiency.

Cost is not the only differentiator, though. Customers always appreciate courteous, personal service. But to really impress their customers, organizations will need to prove that they know their customers and can even anticipate the needs of those customers. Customer knowledge becomes manifest when an employee engages with a customer or when technology uses its knowledge of the customer to create a more personalized experience (see Figure 4.3, How Companies Use Customer Information).

The key is aligning data with strategy, whether this means learning about customers and engaging them or learning about cost structures. For some organizations, their customer insights and data will be a source of value in and of themselves, allowing each company to create new lines of business around its knowledge of customers, markets, or operations.

Moving from insight to action

Discovering something new in a data set is interesting, but it is not impactful unless the organization incorporates that insight into how it does business. Even when systems are well-integrated in the back office and businesses can keep up with the proliferation of new data, transforming that information into useful, actionable business intelligence can be a challenge. It depends on a combination of data access, easy-to-use tools, and people who are able to ask the right questions, spot the relevant trends, draw the right conclusions, and get others to take action. The Illinois Department of Transportation used this combination of tools and techniques to optimize highway salt procurement and reduce fatal accidents (see IDOT: Data Self-Service Saves Lives).

IDOT: Data Self-Service Saves Lives

The Illinois Department of Transportation (IDOT) ran into roadblocks from having its data trapped in siloed legacy systems. Unable to match roadway, inventory, and financial information, IDOT bought salt by guesswork—and found itself with either not enough salt to clear roads of snow or too much salt on hand when winter ended.

IDOT implemented a comprehensive business intelligence platform—a one-stop information shop—connecting the systems. Staff can now view information through dashboards and portals, in addition to crunching the data, without help from the IT department.

The result: a new "salt usage dashboard" that makes sure each part of the state has the right amount of salt. And, with "self-service" access to data, staff members are uncovering new insights, such as determining the real reasons for fatal accidents that were previously classified under the meaningless catch-all "other." This knowledge has led to training for police officers who have prevented accidents and saved lives.

With the wealth of data available, keeping a tight rein on business intelligence is not the right choice. New tools democratize business intelligence, permitting ever widening circles of people to use the resulting knowledge to the company's benefit.

Business intelligence needs to be integrated with collaboration so that the right people and the right processes can leverage the new insight. By bringing business data together with technologies that people already use—including spreadsheets, e-mail, and shared workspaces—organizations can adopt business intelligence solutions across a wide cross-section of their employees. The benefits of

Companies that have a high use of business intelligence make the
tools easy to use with familiar technology.

(% of companies reporting high use of BI and actions taken to accelerate usage)

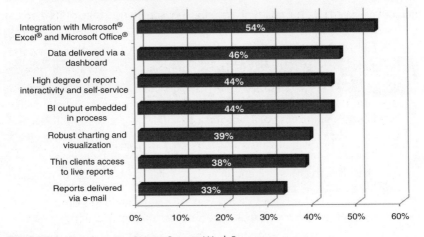

FIGURE 4.4   Incorporating BI into Current Work Processes
Source: Survey of 678 companies by TDWI

collaboration will extend beyond the team responsible for the data or the
function (see Figure 4.4, Incorporating BI into Current Work Processes).

Turning transparency into an opportunity

Regulations such as Sarbanes-Oxley and Basel II require organizations
to make more of their operating data available to the public and to
regulatory agencies, often forcing them to rethink their internal systems to reach compliance. The same is true of reporting concepts like
Triple Bottom Line and International Financial Reporting Standards
(IFRS). Regulatory mandates condition businesses to see transparency
as a challenge and a burden, but transparency can be an opportunity
to better understand the operating environment and create new value,
as Nypro, a global plastics manufacturer, did in using compliance data
to better serve customers (see Nypro: Finding Profits in Transparency).
As business relationships become closer, organizations are negotiating
partnerships that expose more of their internal operations to partners
they trust. Organizations may take this opportunity to examine their
internal processes and find meaningful patterns in their data.

Nypro: Finding Profits in Transparency

Global plastics manufacturer Nypro must ensure every stage of its medical device production process is managed and recorded according to U.S. Food and Drug Administration requirements. The Clinton, Massachusetts, company's new Web-based business intelligence and statistical process control software technology also proved beneficial to the sales teams. They can use the data to prove to existing and potential customers that Nypro consistently works to specification.

"Increasingly, customers want to verify that their product complies with specified requirements and check the status of their product development online," says Michael Kilday, corporate director of Quality Assurance and Regulatory Affairs at Nypro. "Now that we can provide this option, it will become part of the Nypro experience for current and potential customers."

Another added benefit: The system identifies problems faster, allowing the company to save $8 million per year in product scrap.

Work Effectively in a Collaborative Environment

The complexities of data and changing business models are replicated at the micro level by the increasingly demanding nature of information work. People whose job roles were previously structured and segmented are now drawn into a more transparent, collaborative world of work where they are expected to incorporate volumes of new data and new channels of communication seamlessly into their daily routines. Sometimes the growing complexity of the information work environment—the sheer number of tools and technologies required to perform simple tasks—can overwhelm people whose expertise is in the work, not in software skills. New innovations in information work software are finally beginning to reverse the trends of complexity, in part by giving people easier and more consistent ways to integrate common work tasks and data sources into a more simple, unified work experience.

Analyzing networks of people, not just data

Data is only valuable if the insights derived from it can be applied by people in the organization. In the rush to champion the power of quantitative thinking and data systems, it is easy to overlook the decisive role that human insight still plays. The data may be shouting insights and knowledge, but it might as well be silent if the right people are not there to listen. As Yaneer Bar-Yam, head of the New England Complex Systems Institute in Cambridge, Massachusetts, says: "One of the most profound results of complex systems research is that when systems are highly complex, individuals matter."[3]

People are also critical inputs to business intelligence when they form "human sensor networks" to rally around a political issue, save a television show from cancelation, or provide feedback and share information on products. One example of human sensor networks comes from the San Diego fires of 2007, where cell phones, Internet search, online discussion groups, text messages, Web forums, blogs, and photo sharing kept the community and rescue workers informed about the fire at a level of detail that would not have been possible without technology.[4]

Modeling human behavior to drive business decisions

Statistical sampling techniques can forecast the behavior of everyone from air travelers to Web surfers to baseball players. For example, it may not be immediately obvious that demand for foods like Pop-Tarts will spike in the wake of a natural disaster, but Wal-Mart has data showing that this is true and, consequently, keeps plenty of inventories in the pipeline during hurricane season in the southeastern United States.[5]

Procter & Gamble, during its acquisition of Gillette, spent over a year analyzing data and found that supply chain, workforce, and customer synergies were factors in determining the price P&G would pay for Gillette.[6] Indeed, companies as diverse as Amazon, Lowe's, and Harrah's use information gleaned from customer transactions to anticipate customer preferences. This approach helps these companies and others like them develop effective responses to recover at-risk customer relationships and reduce turnover costs.

Visualizing relationships

Relationship mapping software enables the visual representation of relationships and influence within organizations. People appear as circles of larger or smaller size depending on their influence, with lines of connection to various points at varying degrees of thickness depending on the strength of the connection. These maps provide greater insight into the true patterns of communication within a group than the traditional organization chart, and they can be a valuable tool in managing human resources.[7]

Managing interruptions and staying productive

Information workers are swamped with e-mail, instant messages, text messages, online meetings, RSS feeds, project workflow notifications, team workspaces, blogs, and social networks. The ongoing question is how to stay up to date with useful communications technologies without being overwhelmed by them. A study at the Institute for the Future of the Mind at Oxford University found that people of all ages have a hard time refocusing on highly cognitive work after being interrupted. That means companies need to manage interruptions just as they manage the other parts of a task, such as content, data, and project plans.

There is no uniform opinion about the best ways to work in an information-rich environment. Although some senior managers assume from their own experiences that it is easier to work without distractions, people accustomed to multitasking may prefer a dynamic workstyle to stay engaged even at the expense of productivity. Also, interruptions sometimes lead to more opportunities. For example, is a sales representative creating more value by filling in a monthly expense report or answering an instant message that turns out to be a hot lead on a new order, but interrupts him in the middle of that task?

It is important that the IT infrastructure be flexible enough to rapidly incorporate new forms of communication without disturbing the core business functions or threatening security or privacy. The way to stay productive in an information-rich environment is to adopt a platform that permits a secure and managed core while facilitating adaptation at the edge, where employees and customers meet, process meets process, and requirement meets requirement. Here, exceptions and change move too fast for core systems, but people can quickly adapt to whatever they encounter.

STRATEGIC TECHNOLOGIES TO DRIVE INSIGHTS

The following technologies can help organizations gather data from diverse sources and use it to drive business insights that lead to competitive advantage while not disrupting workers' concentration and workflow:

Business intelligence and analytics to make data accessible and useful to people in their roles.

Open data sources to allow businesses and consumers to map proprietary data against licensed or public data.

Unified collaboration platform to simplify the way people interact and share data.

Scalable data architecture to simplify the incorporation of new sources and types of data.

Five Tools for Turning Complexity into Insight

The business intelligence and analytics tools that companies use to turn complexity into insight fall into five classes: enterprise systems, analytic technologies, business data in portals and information work applications, visualization, and simulation.

1. **Enterprise systems:** Customer-facing workers, such as sales professionals, customer service representatives, retail associates, or service providers, all benefit from business data that allows them to anticipate and exceed customer expectations in any given transaction. Customer relationship management (CRM) can point toward not only effective strategies for delivering personalized service, but also up-sell and cross-sell opportunities that even seasoned sales professionals might miss. CRM data should be easily available in the applications that people know and use, such as the

e-mail or unified communications client, so that the information will be at the worker's fingertips when the customer calls.

2. **Analytical technologies:** Core technologies to analyze data include spreadsheets, online analytical processors (OLAP), statistical and quantitative algorithms, rules engines, data mining tools, text mining tools, and simulation tools. Emerging technologies, including categorization, genetic algorithms, audio and video mining, swarm intelligence, and information extraction tools, will greatly enhance traditional tools.[8]

3. **Business data in portals and information work applications:** In an Economist Business Unit study of CFOs sponsored by Microsoft, nearly 64 percent of respondents cited "ready access to data" as the most important contributor to finance empowerment. Portals make business data readily available to people in all roles, allowing them and their teams to quickly align their efforts to the strategic goals of the business. In addition, workers can make better use of enterprise data by bringing it seamlessly into the familiar desktop applications that they use for financial management and visualization, such as Microsoft Excel spreadsheet software, so they do not have to disrupt tried-and-true work practices.

4. **Visualization:** Reports do not easily represent multidimensional relationships, and even less complex relationships can be more easily seen than read about. Data visualization plays an important role in understanding social systems, adding views into processes and customer relationships—not to mention the social, economic, and political relationships that organizations must track to remain cognizant of their operating environment. Think of a heads-up display, for example, which provides a fighter pilot with a steady stream of representations of critical systems in a form that is immediately intelligible. This same kind of approach is now being integrated into workstations for financial analysts, whose information landscape is nearly as complex and dynamic as the cockpit of a jet plane. The utility of visualization tools depends on their ability to use the available dimensions (line, shape, color, and movement

over time) to represent complex and dynamic systems in ways that reveal meaning without overwhelming the viewer with sensory overload.

British Petroleum, for example, found visualization tools vital for emergency preparedness in the event of hurricanes and other natural disasters (see British Petroleum: A New View Prevents Disaster).

British Petroleum: A New View Prevents Disaster

As Hurricane Katrina developed, British Petroleum (BP) officials spent hours furiously pulling data manually from 20 databases and Web-based sources to locate and help all their people in the danger zone. After the crisis, the oil giant—headquartered in London—wanted a better system for handling emergencies.

BP developed a Hurricane Management System, which combines 3D satellite imagery and real-time weather data with symbols that represent BP's people and assets. The highly visual representation allows crisis managers to see weather patterns—and to calculate their potential impact on people and facilities more clearly, accurately, and quickly. BP can also overlay outside feeds of traffic and housing information to speed planning and aid.

"You pan in and look at your data, and it just happens," says Stephen Fortune, an information management director at BP. "When we're in crisis mode, people can't wait for technology to catch up. Even a delay of 30 seconds represents a loss of valuable time."

5. **Simulations:** Business process owners have long simulated everything from customer queues at amusement parks to the flow of material through a Lean manufacturing operation. Now, the ability to combine rich and complex data from multiple sources makes it possible to use simulations to test assumptions against an array of variables that more closely match the dynamics and uncertainties of the real world. High quality data and powerful

systems can run simulations over and over again to perform regression analysis, which can take the guesswork out of identifying risks and probabilities, and help isolate the factors that make a real difference in outcomes. People will not *know* the future, but they will have precise information on the distribution of uncertainties, which can lead to decisions that better balance risk and reward.

Over the next decade, simulation data will likely combine with experiential and sensory data to create even more complex environments. Gaming skills will become a mainstream business competency as organizations attempt to anticipate the outcomes of complex business relationships, using both realistic and abstract simulation environments.

Open Data Sources

Although data sources in isolation can be useful, their value increases significantly when combined with other data. Imagine, for example, modeling the land holdings of a large agricultural organization in combination with weather data to find the optimal place to plant a new hybrid and take maximum advantage of its yield characteristics.

More data sources are coming online all the time, as techniques for measurement of granular processes get better and the costs of storing large volumes of data approach trivial levels. Some online game communities that open their application programming interfaces (APIs) have hundreds of developers who share their creative talents with the community, allowing people to download everything from starships to avatars. The exchange of data for business applications will soon be just as brisk.

Unified Collaboration Platforms Reduce Complexity

Unified communications and collaboration help reduce the complexity of people-based interactions, especially as the proliferation of new channels threatens to overwhelm people's attention spans and ability to focus.

Single communication client

Giving people a single point of entry across the myriad ways of communicating via technology makes work a lot simpler, for both end users and IT. Unified communications brings together voice-based telephony, Voice over IP (VoIP), fax, e-mail, instant messaging, calendaring and meeting requests, contact information, and team memberships into a single application that is available across applications, platforms, and devices. As unified communications evolves, it will provide a common platform for managing multiple social networks and user profiles, reducing the overhead that many people currently experience when participating in different online environments.

Presence awareness

One of the most useful features of unified communications is presence awareness, which lets people see at a glance the availability of others in their network. This capability is especially useful when presence is integrated automatically with personal and group calendars and telephony systems. Awareness not only makes it easier to choose the right mode of communication (for example, send e-mail if the person is away, call or instant message if the person is online and not busy), it also lets people control their exposure to interruptions according to their personal preferences and priorities. Monsanto found presence awareness particularly useful to maintain employee productivity when implementing flexible schedules and work-at-home programs (see Monsanto: Instant Presence Brings Instant Benefits).

Monsanto: Instant Presence Brings Instant Benefits

Monsanto instituted flexible hours and work-at-home programs to ease the strain on employees when a major highway underwent significant repairs near its 28-building headquarters in St. Louis. The agricultural biotechnology giant turned to a unified communications platform, with presence awareness capabilities, to ensure that employees could collaborate just as well under the new work scenarios.

When employees are logged on to the virtual private network, remote employees can see who is online and available for a quick instant messaging conversation. "The system makes internal communication more agile and our lives much easier," says Aarti Shah, a supply chain generalist with Monsanto. "It increases our efficiency and productivity by cutting down response times for quick feedback and resolutions to issues. I already see a difference in the way I work, because the system helps me to multitask and to discuss current activities with various team members, so that I can get better results and make smarter decisions."

Subscription-based content

Subscription-based content enables people to control and personalize their window into the wider world of information. RSS and Atom feeds aggregate content published by Web sites, blogs, document repositories, team workspaces, and business applications that can be consumed in a browser, e-mail client, mobile device, or information work application. Podcasts do the same for rich-media content. As a result, a lot of the complexities associated with keeping up to date in an information-rich environment will disappear, allowing people to focus on information that is relevant to their roles and interests.

Insight Requires a Scalable Data Architecture

Data cannot be turned into insight without a robust architecture that encompasses data warehouses, a service-oriented architecture (SOA), and metadata.

Data warehouse

Simplifying the end-user environment depends on back-end data systems that can interoperate easily and pass data along in standard formats. Those systems include not only structured database applications and business data stores but also collaboration data (from e-mail, real-time communication systems, shared workspaces, social networks, and discussion groups), documents, and information from the hard drives of PCs connected to the enterprise network. Legacy data can be incorporated into the data warehouse through custom integration or specialized servers that translate between proprietary and standard formats. Paper-based data can be captured in digital format using optical character recognition assisted by statistical algorithms that learn and adapt to reduce errors. Other structured data can be captured at the front end of processes using digital forms that are easily designed by nontechnical users and then deployed to the Web, Tablet PCs, or mobile devices. Eventually, traditional paper and writing will find a comfortable means of capturing information in a digital repository.

Service-oriented architecture

A service-oriented architecture (SOA) enables the interchange of information across the enterprise as a "service" that can be consumed or exposed in a common framework, such as a portal or desktop application, without requiring a dedicated client. An SOA makes it faster and easier to develop integrated, composite applications that can use data within the system in innovative ways.

Metadata

In addition to the primary data, the unified logical repository should include metadata descriptions that make information visible to search engines in a variety of contexts. Metadata is also necessary to trace patterns of communication and collaboration that can then be visualized as relationship maps and to connect individual people within the network to the information, documents, and processes with which they are involved. Eventually, metadata will include security and access policies for individual documents and records; document histories including authorship, revisions, and chains of custody for auditing purposes; and dynamic descriptions that push data out when it "wants" to be found in a particular context, rather than waiting to be discovered with the right search engine query.

TENETS FOR SUCCESS

The ability to gain insights from complexity is critical to the success of all organizations. IT is a strategic enabler of that success. Decisions about platforms, applications, and end-user environments matter—not just because they affect costs but because they can provide the capabilities, speed, and choices businesses need to compete in an uncertain world.

In a world of exponential increases in the volume of data and a competitive requirement to draw the right conclusions from that information, software adds value by assisting people and businesses in determining the right course of action. Companies seeking effective IT solutions for information overload and business intelligence should consider the following approaches:

Make data strategic and trustworthy. Data scattered across multiple repositories and silos is hard to marshal for business value, and it makes people the point of integration across different systems and applications. Undervaluing the data is an even bigger problem. When data systems are integrated in the back office using a framework that enables interoperability and easy interchange between servers, client applications, and the Web, the infrastructure investment pays off by simplifying access for people and increasing the chances for insight.

Make software the communication hub. Unified communications technology makes software a central communication platform, capable of integrating voice, data, and real-time and asynchronous media in a single, simplified view for people. When other collaboration tools have access to presence information, so that people see who is immediately available, communication and collaboration can be more effective and timely.

Access data through productivity applications. Pervasive access to information when, where, and how it is needed, along with easy-to-use tools to glean insights from data are a foundation for confident decision-making across all levels of an organization. These applications are especially critical in customer-facing environments, where access to data can be the difference in delivering outstanding service or closing a sale.

Make analytics ubiquitous. Organizations that give analytics and data access to only a few analysts risk not asking the right questions at the right time and missing the opportunity to take advantage of the insights hiding in data. Companies need to open up access to data and analytic tools, both by providing technology facilities (such as workspaces and community sites for discussion of business data) and the cultural and management practices to encourage inquiry and exploration.

SOURCES OF INSIGHT

If you focus on the data coming from the following sources, you will gain insight into your business, your customers, and the world.

Data Source	What You Can Learn
Subscription Data	From watching global events to discovering trends to listening to customers, text mining on RSS feeds can provide a wide range of insight from communities of bloggers, newswires, and other sources.
Business Processes	Business processes that have been automated are a great source of insight. Trends hidden in the databases beneath these systems can unlock where and how processes go wrong or where costs are coming from.
Enterprise Systems	Systems across the organization—from financial to manufacturing to human resources to R&D—are all data-rich learning environments, where applying the right analytics can generate insights that will drive business performance, retain employees, and discover new products and services.
Instruments and Devices	More commonplace tools, instruments, and devices are becoming data-enabled and network-enabled. For example, telematics systems in vehicles, RFID tags, digital medical equipment, smart dust, digital tools, and instruments in industry and design provide precise measurements of formerly "analog" processes, which can then be factored in to data-driven strategies and decisions. Many physical objects in the future will come with, or be represented by, metadata.
Public Data	Many organizations, such as the United Nations, the World Bank, and the Organization for Economic Co-operation and Development, provide external data that can give insights into demographics and markets. Most governments are also rich repositories of data.

NOTES

1. For more information on FareCast's business model, see http://www.farecast .com/about/ourTechnology

2. Buchanan, Mark. "Sin Cities: The Geometry of Crime." *New Scientist*, April 30, 2008. http://www.newscientist.com/article.ns?id=mg19826541.000&print=true

3. McKenzi, Dobora. "Will a Pandemic Bring Down Civilization?" *New Scientist*, April 5, 2008. http://www.newscientist.com/article.ns?id=mg19826501.400&print= true

4. Palmer, Jason. "Emergency 2.0 is Coming to a Web Site Near You." *New Scientist*, May 2, 2008. http://technology.newscientist.com/article.ns?id=mg19826545.900 &print=true

5. Example cited in Ayres, Ian. *Super Crunchers: Why Thinking by the Numbers is the New Way to be Smart*. New York: Bantam, 2007.

6. Davenport, Thomas H. and Harris, J. *Competing on Analytics*. Boston, MA: Harvard Business School Press, 2007.

7. Hindo, Brian. "Mapping the Crowd." *BusinessWeek*, November 15, 2007. http:// www.businessweek.com/innovate/content/nov2007/id20071114_879795.htm?chan= innovation_special+report+-+in_in

8. Davenport, Thomas H. and Harris, J. *Competing on Analytics*. Boston, MA: Harvard Business School Press, 2007.

CHAPTER 5

Building Strategic Advantage Through IT

cross industries, information technology (IT) budgets as a percentage of sales hover just below 4 percent. IT expenditures are a significant cost for most organizations. But many still struggle to effectively account for their return on IT investments, either in reduced costs or in differentiated value to their customers. One of the biggest problems in justifying IT budgets is the growth of the knowledge economy: Our economics remain rooted in Industrial Age terms that measure productivity strictly in terms of inputs and outputs. When the only framework is industrial economics, everything looks like a production line. However, innovations in information work technology are increasingly rendering this metric insufficient to gauge the true amount of value creation in organizations whose "outputs" include innovation, high-value customer relationships, strategic alignment of partners, and internal fluidity of knowledge. Outcomes, not outputs, are the new standard of performance, and our methods of measuring the value of IT in that context need to evolve accordingly.

The most common strategies for understanding and accepting IT investments include the competitive "cost of doing business" argument, followed quickly—and not surprisingly, given the previously stated position—by the attachment of technology to a process. There is nothing wrong with either approach, but neither helps IT managers connect spending to a business outcome in a tangible way.

Information technology becomes a strategic asset when it makes the entire business adaptive and ready for change by connecting people, process, and information to drive results. How an organization measures the results of its technology investments is important, because the continuous improvement of any function requires a clear way to measure performance against goals. The strategic value of IT, therefore, becomes clearer when executives move away from Industrial Age metrics and toward a more holistic assessment of "return on knowledge."

In fact, better measurement of the return on IT investments can yield strong overall financial returns. Companies that excel at managing the value of their IT investments outpace their peers in overall financial performance, according to research by The Hackett Group. Essentially, Hackett says, companies that better manage the business value of IT—including governance, portfolio management, and other IT management tactics—have 49 percent higher net profitability than their peer group. In addition, their return on equity and return on assets are higher (see Figure 5.1: The Financial Proof: The Right IT Delivers Strategic Advantage).

THE CHALLENGE OF MEASURING RETURN ON KNOWLEDGE

There is a growing disconnect between traditional accounting methods for returns and those for returns that are now known as *intangibles*. To address this issue, Microsoft has invested in the Institute for Innovation and Information Productivity (IIIP), a trade association (www.iii-p.org) charged with exploring alternative economic models that better reflect the nature of the knowledge economy.

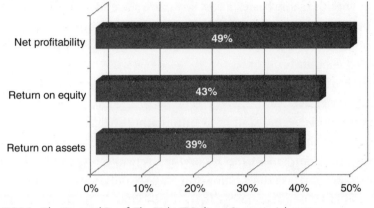

(% "top IT value performers" exceeded their peer group in specific financial metrics)

FIGURE 5.1   The Financial Proof: The Right IT Delivers Strategic Advantage
Source: The Hackett Group, 2008 (http://www.thehackettgroup.com/studies/itbvminsight/)

Although the Institute strives to present a reasoning process that managers may find useful, it does not reflect a definitive methodology for anticipating value. In fact, one of the Institute's primary positions is that some horizontal technology cannot be justified using traditional accounting methods. That said, the challenges of accounting do not imply that IT has no value. Rather, it is that the economics of the Knowledge Age have not caught up with innovation. We hope that the research derived from our investment in the IIIP will accelerate other research that will in turn create working methods to help CIOs and other managers gain a better understanding of the return on knowledge.

WHY IT MATTERS

The strategic value of information technology has been a controversial subject in business literature over the past several years. Consultant and author Nicholas Carr famously asked, "Does IT Matter?" because he observed that infrastructure and software are commodities, equally available to every competitor in the market.[1] In his view, the data center is—at best—a cost of doing business, and a company would be better served if it could reduce its IT footprint.

Carr's question is a bit misleading. The central issue is not the value IT generally speaking, but its application within the business. Two companies with the same basic IT cost structure can end up in very different competitive positions, depending on whether they are leveraging their information assets to facilitate agility or seeking efficiency through business process optimization.

Carr's observations may ring true for some organizations that invested heavily in custom-built, rigid enterprise systems, which they expected to confer value simply by automating structured processes. *Of course* the value of those systems is limited: No process can be reduced to zero cost. Companies cannot save their way into prosperity as a long-term strategy. At a certain point, innovation and growth are necessary, and rigid IT systems are more often an inhibitor, rather than an enabler, of change. In fact, when change is necessary, enterprises that adopt a static approach may be hostages of the IT providers, system integrators, and services organizations that hold a monopoly on the skills required to update their business rules. Those costs can rapidly escalate, eroding the hoped-for benefits from process optimization. How an organization defines value is a key component of how it realizes value. For IT that means aligning investments with strategy. This process ensures the results line up with goals that are larger than any single technology, application, or system.

In cases where static IT systems impede agility, it is more accurate to say that the *implementation strategy* was the problem, not the concept of IT or its ownership. IT does not have to be rigid and purpose-built around static workflows. IT that is focused on flexibility, end-user productivity, and extensibility can offer the same short-term efficiencies as more structured workflow solutions, but at lower cost and greater long-term business value. Flexible IT adapts to change without requiring constant changes to the deep rules and schemas that reflect current realities.

For example, the limitations of a more rigid infrastructure drove MTV Networks to invest in a new intranet portal that would allow users to publish their own content (see MTV Wants Easy Access to Its Next Big Idea).

MTV Wants Easy Access to Its Next Big Idea

MTV Networks advocates, even relies on, the free flow of ideas and content to keep a fresh, hip perspective and to respond to an ever-changing viewing audience. "In our business, success is all about creativity—about coming up with the next big idea," says Dave Mitchell, vice president of Application Development at MTV Networks, a division of New York City-based global entertainment content company Viacom. "To stay in touch with our audiences, we need to constantly reinvent ourselves, which means taking peoples' ideas and making them part of a greater knowledge pool."

Unfortunately, MTV's portal infrastructure did not allow users to publish their own content. A new portal based on a collaboration server empowered users to self-publish. The rich collaboration tools of the new portal enabled communications and boosted productivity at the network.

"Today we can collaborate globally, not only on the sharing of content but also on how that content is created," says Joe Simon, senior vice president and CIO at MTV Networks. "By working in this manner, both time-to-market and costs are reduced, which means we can produce more content for the same amount of dollars. And in our business, the more content we can produce, the greater our chances of creating a hit."

Source: http://www.microsoft.com/casestudies/casestudy.aspx?casestudyid= 4000002398

Erik Brynjolfsson, the director of MIT's Center for eBusiness, agrees that it is important to surround innovative IT with the right practices and culture. "Whether IT improves productivity depends primarily on the complementary organizational investments that companies make in addition to their IT investments."[2] While Carr says the downfall of IT is due to the fact that companies can rapidly copy "commodity" solutions in the marketplace, Brynjolfsson argues that IT alone is not a competitive differentiator. An effective information technology investment reflects the organization's complex values, social structure, process, and practice. For another organization to copy just the technology would create discord, not an advantage.

WHY APPLICATIONS MATTER

For most managers, business applications are the windows into information technology. For CFOs, the primary entry point is probably the financial management system and its related compliance features. For the vice president of sales, the customer relationship management (CRM) system and its accompanying reporting system for sales performance reign supreme.

William Blundon of Boston-based Extraprise Group Inc., recommends that all implementation projects be driven by a business case.[3] This advice is important, because the business case is much more than a return on investment. It is a contextual plan for how value is determined within an organization. The finances may be part of a business case, but as Washington Mutual CIO Jerry Gross states in his book *In Search of Business Value:*[4]

> Return on investment of technology is a very good financial metric to shoot for, and we've done that. But we also have some non-financial or intangible metrics... The people part is all about the behavioral. Whether the end user is an employee or a customer, do you see a behavioral change?

The business case reflects the anticipated results of investments. If an investment does not match or exceed one of its primary metrics, then advocates will have a difficult time defending it.

Project managers need to distinguish between false metrics and real business metrics. False metrics count things and profess progress but have little meaning if they are not applied to the overall goal. In CRM systems, for example, "contactable customers" is a false metric, as is the number of documents in a knowledge management system. Both count progress, and perhaps use, but neither metric ties to tangible results such as higher revenue or market share. They are intermediary metrics, their results (the existence of data) meaningless until applied, for instance, to convert a contactable lead into a sale. Figure 5.2 shows examples of results-oriented business metrics.

Whatever metrics an organization holds most closely are the ones that drive the value conversation. These metrics are usually defined by

Business Goal	Desired Outcome	Metric
Customer retention	Customer satisfaction	Market share
Profitability	Cash flow	Sales backlog
Cycle-time reductions	Quality index	Rework
Productivity	Percent of revenue from new products	Organizational competency/skill levels
R&D conversion	New products and services, first-mover advantage	Pricing power, market growth

FIGURE 5.2   Examples of Results-Oriented Business Metrics

the company's strategy, and they exist as inputs from conversations with the board of directors about shareholder value. Many business results are not pure metrics but indexes, such as quality being a combination of manufacturing quality, returns, call center calls, delivery issues, and other factors that reflect overall quality, rather than quality at any one operation. In the previous CRM example, sales backlog and market share may be key. But if the issue is pipeline efficiency, then cycle-time reduction around contacts and contracts may prove a more relevant metric.

At Service Repair Solutions, the key productivity metric was time per call, which its previous CRM solution did not allow the company to track adequately (see Less Time, Better Service).

Less Time, Better Service

As Las Vegas–based Service Repair Solutions Inc., discovered, not all customer relationship management metrics are created equal, and neither are all CRM systems. The company, which offers solutions to help automotive

(continued)

technicians increase the efficiency and accuracy of their work, puts a lot of stock in ensuring that its call center representatives not only meet customer needs but do so efficiently. But Service Repair Solutions' CRM system did not integrate into its other systems well, leaving customer service reps without all the information necessary to serve customers. As a result, reps were spending too much time on each call without necessarily meeting the customer's needs.

Moving to a new CRM system, which was better integrated with the company's other systems, had dramatic benefits—reducing call times by 30 percent. In addition, the new integrated application reduced training time for new call center agents by 25 percent. Agents can now accommodate more calls and offer better customer service, according to CIO Jeff Hislop.

Source: http://www.microsoft.com/casestudies/casestudy.aspx? casestudyid=4000002448

WHY PLATFORMS MATTER

Information technology adds strategic value when it can change with the business. Because change happens most quickly at the operational edge of the enterprise and not at the bureaucratic center, the ideal IT model pushes out most capabilities to business users by giving them easy ways to customize their information environment and modify processes as their needs and roles evolve. The best solutions also deliver a common platform, so system operation and the data each user has access to are consistent and familiar across the experience. The way features work should be well known, so knowledge workers can concentrate on work, rather than on an application's arcane syntax or iconography.

This approach leaves IT management the essential task of governing platform policies, security, access control, and overall strategy, without taxing their resources and turning IT into a bottleneck of business change. It means IT drives standardization and leverages economies of scale, rather than simply automating structured processes. A rigid IT infrastructure, on the other hand, locks the business in to a fixed set of practices, one that may have been optimized according to a snapshot of business needs taken years before the solution is fully implemented.

1. Make proactivity a rule of thumb

2. Better manage change

3. Implement and enforce policies

4. Improve relationships and information exchange with senior management

5. Establish IT managers as strategic advisors outside of the traditional realm of IT

FIGURE 5.3   Five Steps to Strategic IT Management

Source: ESJ.com column by Dave R. Taylor, based on interviews of 500 enterprise IT managers by Dynamic Markets (http://esj.com/enterprise/article.aspx?EditorialsID=2090)

When business groups or individual users try to change the outdated process, the cost in IT resources is often prohibitive. The result is that the business is slower to respond and, therefore, less able to compete with more nimble players in the market.

A platform is also important in the management of complexity. Well-designed platforms minimize the need for users or developers to think about how things work within an environment. They offer a common way to introduce features that may be complex, but provide a natural bridge from existing knowledge because of their relationship to the platform

According to a survey and analysis by Dynamic Markets, IT managers can assume a stronger role in making information technology strategic within their organizations by adopting five tactics (see Figure 5.3, Five Steps to Strategic IT Management).

Empowering People at the Point of Change

Flexibility is critical to any process, and it is most valuable in handling exceptions. For example, service escalations that occur when a customer's problem falls outside of the parameters the process is designed to handle. In those cases, the ability to execute rests with the person, not the process. Too often, however, the abilities of people in a "structured" service role are constrained by the limitations of their tools. Practices that discourage individual initiative also diminish the ability of employees to add value to a transaction, which can result in reduced customer satisfaction or missed opportunities.

After concerted sales and marketing efforts to boost growth, Lincoln Heritage Funeral Planning found that its outdated systems made it impossible for customer service staff to keep up with and prioritize sales leads (see LHFP Arms Customer Service Reps to Prioritize, Report on Leads).

LHFP Arms Customer Service Reps to Prioritize, Report on Leads

As accelerated sales and marketing efforts grew business for Lincoln Heritage Funeral Planning (LHFP), it was apparent that its customer relationship management system was overworked and lacked the ability to fully support processes such as lead distribution, reporting, appointment dispatching, and appointment confirmation. Also, sales staff in the Portland, Oregon, company's call center did not have a way to effectively prioritize calls or find information on leads. Upgrading its CRM system, coupled with a custom caller application and migrating to a newer database platform, helped the company streamline both processes and reporting.

Source: http://www.microsoft.com/casestudies/casestudy.aspx?casestudyid=4000002454

In a fast-changing world where exceptions occur more frequently, are harder to foresee, and have far-ranging repercussions for the business, there is no such thing as a "low-value" or "structured information work" role. Organizations can empower employees to succeed in those cases by giving them IT capabilities beyond those of structured systems, such as communications tools (e-mail, instant messaging, Voice over IP), document authoring tools (word processors, spreadsheets, design), and access to user-created content (shared workspaces, communities of practice, blogs, wikis, search results). Beyond that, empowered employees should also have the tools to rapidly disseminate their learning from an exception across the organization, so that it can be more easily dealt with until the more structured systems catch up. Today, every worker needs a flexible, powerful, and connected information work platform and the skills to use it in a variety of contexts and business scenarios.

Coordinating Unstructured tasks

Much of an organization's day-to-day work is done in informal groups. These teams face daily challenges of coordinating members' activities, reviewing documents, managing projects, and performing basic information tasks. Everyone recognizes the aggregate benefits of better coordination among these routine, low-value tasks. Because this work is not specialized and each task is different enough to require a high degree of customization for each user and occurrence, the ROI of custom development to automate such tasks is prohibitive. Also, this work is properly the responsibility of the business unit, not IT, which should instead provide governance over the entire infrastructure.

Extensible application platforms provide an elegant solution. They offer the core functionality that business users need to perform high-level information work individually and in groups. These platforms also provide a way for people to design and deploy customized solutions to automate common tasks that fall between the cracks of enterprise IT solutions.

Facilitating Strategic Change

Sometimes, strategic changes to the business model or unexpected market conditions require IT systems to be modified beyond the scope of expert end users or in-house IT departments. When professional developers or system integrators need to implement new capabilities, several factors impact the speed and cost of deployment. One factor is the support for software development, which depends on the sophistication of the tools developers use to write code and the knowledge resources available through the platform vendor, professional organizations, online communities, and informal channels. Another factor is the extent to which diverse applications within the data center adhere to broadly accepted industry standards. When a platform is widely adopted, it tends to be well-supported by a large ecosystem of developers. As a result, business customers have a wide range of options and a competitive market from which to choose. For example, Helio was able to incorporate new e-mail features into its global offerings in just nine months, thanks to the availability and adoption of widely used technologies (see Helio Flies Higher).

Helio Flies Higher

A Los Angeles-based joint venture between EarthLink and South Korean carrier SK Telecom that offers a range of advanced voice and data services to consumers, Helio prides itself on keeping one step ahead of user demand. Using a widely accepted e-mail technology for mobile device users, Helio was able to create a service that enabled it to offer new services for its customers, such as its "All-in-One" plans, and to support a wide variety of high-end devices. An offer for a 60-day free trial as an introduction to a $9.99 per month plan immediately met with tremendous success. The new technologies "significantly boosted our potential for increased member acquisition and average revenue per user (ARPU)," says Doug Britt, vice president of Service Management at Helio.

Source: http://www.microsoft.com/casestudies/casestudy.aspx?casestudyid= 4000001517

WHY INFRASTRUCTURE MATTERS

Information technology is no longer monolithic, with programs sitting on a single machine that churns out reports, writes data to tables, and sends information to the screens of information workers. Today's IT systems are distributed, optimized for different functions, highly networked, massively redundant, and strategically interconnected. Because IT matters, we do not want the systems we rely on to fail.

Infrastructure matters because it supports the delivery of value. The infrastructure's servers, networks, user authentication protocols, file encryption, databases, e-mail, shared file systems, instant messaging, and a plethora of other IT tools are the pipes and valves, the storage tanks, and the disposal units of information. Often, the infrastructure is abstracted from the business. When the server farm needs to be upgraded to support new processes because the servers are old and need to be replaced, for example, the value justification can sound like IT simply wanting new toys.

To avoid that perception, IT needs to say: *X number of millions of dollars of business runs through our server farms. The mean time between failure is increasing to the point that by X date, we will have X number of business disruptions. Beyond that, our competition—given our current analysis of their online performance metrics—has demonstrated its ability to close a sale 32 percent faster than we can. It may be software, but we suspect that they have upgraded their servers. **That means their customers will have a better experience than ours, and our competitors will gain market share.***

The previous paragraph says a lot about how business relates to IT and the associated choices and options. It is also about timing. Replacing older servers to avoid failure, for example, means first understanding failure. So replacing disks may be more important than replacing servers. Everything needs to be discussed, and IT must think before creating budgets or requesting additional funds.

Operational infrastructure matters in a particular way at each company. It depends on the goods or services a company provides to its markets according to service agreements and on the expectations of its customers. The business must make sure that IT knows how to communicate in business terms, and must communicate in those terms. What makes IT matter is often as much about how the business speaks of technology internally as it is what technology does for the business.

For example, a move by Simon & Schuster to replace its aging mainframe has brought a 300 percent increase in business agility and reduced its IT budget by 11 percent, the company says (see Improving the Books).

Improving the Books

Executives at Simon & Schuster needed greater business agility, but the aging mainframe that facilitated its order fulfillment and distribution processes just could not cut it. The New York City-based publisher sells about 262 million books annually, which translates into 1.9 million orders sent out in more than 5,000 truckloads. As the company began to accelerate its business, it was clear that management of fulfillment and distribution was not able to keep up the pace. Moving mainframe applications to a new server architecture has enabled order takers, warehouse workers, and others involved in fulfillment to complete orders more quickly—even those made at the last minute.

According to the publisher, business processes run 300 percent faster and trouble tickets have been reduced by 75 percent after moving to the server architecture. In addition, the company's overall IT costs have dipped 11 percent.

Source: http://www.microsoft.com/casestudies/casestudy.aspx?casestudyid=4000000733

CREATING A DIALOG BETWEEN BUSINESS AND IT

The value of information technology is often lost because IT stays in IT. The pressures businesses face from outside forces and from internal forces, such as employee, customer, and innovation changes, mean that it is critical for IT to align its plans with the organization's strategy, which is the company's competitive differentiation. The only way to successfully execute is to align the external and internal forces with the tools necessary to react, adapt, and navigate them. IT also helps companies gather and understand data, because that data may reveal customer and market insights in the firm's area of expertise. As a result, the business may discover new value for its customers.

All of these links create a need for an ongoing dialog between business and IT, for a common language of business goals and objectives that are tied to information technology investments and their associated value.

This conversation needs to be a dialog, not a monolog. New technologies may lead to new operational opportunities or new relationship models. If the business wants to innovate on multiple levels, it must carefully listen to what IT has to offer. And in this part of the dialog, IT needs to clearly express—in business terms—the connection between the technology options and the potential business value. For example, a database is not just a database. It is a tool to achieve a business goal. Once the database schema is defined and the hidden logic of its execution is coded, it is as specialized as any person working on a specific business function. Just knowing how a database works will not tell a database administrator why it is important for that database to be coded in a particular way. The administrator needs to understand the business value of the database to understand the "why" behind its coding.

Business is a complex interplay of people and process, of expectation and aspiration. Far too many IT projects have failed over the last 30 years because an organization has not been able to appreciate technological innovation. The value of such innovation is in a technology's capability to align to business goals and to provide new or improved value to the business. If the business or the corporate culture is not ready to accept technological innovation, no amount of persuasion will change that fact.

Indeed, many IT managers acknowledge that they have much to learn about the business, according to a 2006 survey of more than 400 respondents from mid-size companies (see Figure 5.4, Closing the IT–Business Gap).

TENETS FOR SUCCESS

Writing in the *Harvard Business Review*, John Seely Brown and John Hegel observe that "IT's economic impact comes from incremental innovations rather than 'big bang' initiatives . . . If done right, these innovations can also reduce the financial risks by generating near-term returns that can help fund subsequent waves of operating initiatives."[5] In other words, organizations can get more from their IT investment by adopting a layered approach, where each new development effort extends the underlying platform of capabilities, rather than sinking

% of respondents who agreed with the following statements:

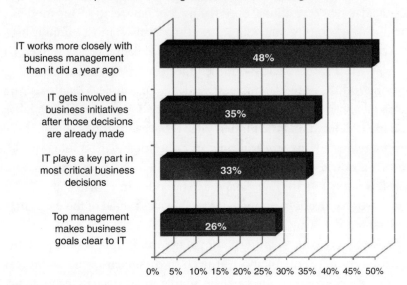

FIGURE 5.4   Closing the IT–Business Gap

Source: Network Computing/InformationWeek (http://www.networkcomputing.com/article/printFull
Article.jhtml?articleID=189400445)

substantial up-front costs into a long-cycle project that does not pay
off until it is complete.

IT is useful; practice is decisive: If every competitor in the market
used the same IT products in the same way, then it would be abso-
lutely legitimate to question the relevance of IT to business strategy.
But every organization is different; each applies its own methods, priorities, and cultural factors to any new business initiative. Nicholas
Carr and his critics agree on one point: All businesses need to focus
on practice innovation—that is, learning and adapting. Technology
can support such innovation when it is flexible, broad-based, and
easy to use. It can also inhibit practice innovation when the technology is glued to static processes, costly to modify, and difficult for
people to learn.

Complex practices drive value in a complex world: The globally
connected business environment never stands still. Complex and

dynamic conditions demand complex and dynamic responses. Process and system standardization creates efficiency but leaves businesses vulnerable in the face of complexity. When organizations are invested in highly standardized, process-based IT systems—whether they are either inside the enterprise or outsourced to a host or provider—people are less able to adapt and respond to new conditions. They are constrained by the limitations of their software tools. When IT enables users to design, deploy, and modify processes that relate to their roles and workload, however, the business is better able to adapt, learn, and grow in a dynamic market.

Agility requires fluidity of people, systems: Rapid change in the wider world creates new roles for people and diminishes the value of established positions. People must be able to adapt quickly and apply their skills and expertise in new contexts. When software is built around a familiar set of basic skills and applications, people can move from role to role more easily. They can reuse their knowledge in a new business context.

The same is true in the data center. When IT systems are designed to integrate around a common framework, IT staff can learn and reuse a basic body of administration and programming knowledge and apply it to many different scenarios. This ability not only increases the productivity and value of IT resources, but motivates IT professionals to deepen their skills, because those skills will be transferable as the technology evolves along a predictable roadmap.

Global businesses require global support: How solutions are delivered should be factored into the strategic value of IT. Globalization is pushing more businesses into unfamiliar markets and creating new competitive conditions. When IT systems need professional development services or support, customers need to know where to turn. A worldwide provider with a tangible commitment to an ecosystem of independent certified partners and experts provides accountability, predictability, choice, and value.

In contrast, national software companies in emerging markets often provide interesting products at attractive prices, especially for domestic customers. But these companies may not be able to offer the long-term support and viability of product development as their customers expand into new markets and demand more complex capabilities. Loose-knit communities of developers, while global in scope and frequently responsive, provide little of the accountability that enterprise customers demand. Nor can they speak to the development roadmaps of their products, because these developers do not know themselves.

Finally, large vendors that derive revenues primarily from professional services and integration do not have the market incentives to deliver out-of-the-box value from the software products they provide. Services organizations make money from service engagements, long-term support agreements, and change orders. They also benefit from a relative scarcity of the skills necessary to service their products in the open market. Such a business model clearly works well for these firms. But it may provide less predictability and value for customers than simply buying licenses for products that meet baseline business needs and can be extended at low marginal cost.

WHY IT STILL MATTERS

You may or may not buy into all of the value arguments presented in this chapter, but you may well have ordered this book using a PC. And you probably have a device for e-mail in your pocket or on your desk. So let us look at e-mail as a valuable technology investment.

Just because everyone has a device for sending and receiving e-mail does not discount it as an effective tool or competitive differentiator. What matters is how your company uses e-mail. If the point is only to answer routine questions, then e-mail probably will not create differentiation in your business' market. On the other hand, if your employees use it to, for example, send photos that capture fashion trends to a shared workspace that promotes collaborative decisions on how to incorporate those trends into your product line, then the value of e-mail moves from a cost-saving application for sending internal memos to one that drives strategic innovation.

EIGHT WAYS TO ACHIEVE MORE STRATEGIC IT

1. **Connect information to the business functions it supports.** From applications to infrastructure, you must understand the value of data and tie it to the IT investment. It is much harder to justify infrastructure or other IT investments in the abstract.

2. **Understand the business and speak the language of business.** IT is too often enamored with acronyms and abbreviations. Businesses have those, too. You must make business models and business language as innate in IT as the department's own models and slang. And always communicate to the business in business language.

3. **Build business expertise.** Although the IT department is expected to be a group of generalists supporting multiple business functions, it is just as important to segment customers and understand where IT needs to invest in expertise, customer support, and so on. Hiring business people within IT who can drive the strategic conversation may be a better investment than switching transaction monitors in terms of adding value.

4. **Tie the IT investment to competitive differentiation.** IT is an extension—and a tool—of the business' strategy. Investments in information technology can only realize value when they deliver on a strategic metric.

5. **Create a dialog with business.** The dialog between business and IT is crucial as a way to facilitate shared learning. It is also about offering a point of view or marketing an idea. Businesses can invest in many areas. If IT truly believes that technology is a viable and more effective use of capital than another area, the group needs to not only talk about it but sell it to business leaders.

6. **Capture value.** A major problem with ROI calculations is that they are done before a project and often abandoned soon after the project is funded. IT departments that want their value recognized need to establish some guidelines for success (even if they are "soft" or nontraditional measurements), monitor the project's return on investment, continue to align and adjust the project, and be honest with the business about the outcomes of technology investments.

7. **Create a learning environment.** As with capturing value, capturing knowledge is important. Initial designs for new systems, practices, and policies may look good on paper, but they may not perform or deliver as expected. By creating a learning environment, where IT and business partner to provide feedback and action plans based on that feedback, businesses have a better opportunity to cut losses and fail fast, and to improve their chances of identifying true innovations that may lead to strategic breakthroughs.

8. **Think about the business implications of systems.** Realizing value does not stop when an application icon shows up on a computer's desktop. Value is created by using technology in the execution of a process or other type of work. People must understand how a new tool fits into their work model. And if it does not fit the model, they need help understanding how the tool can fit. That will empower users to push back and become a part of the feedback system that adjusts tools to better meet real-world business needs.

KEY INFRASTRUCTURE INVESTMENTS FOR COMPETITIVE ADVANTAGE

The following table lists common IT investments and the business rationale that typically underlies their deployment in the enterprise.

Technology	Business Rationale
Process Automation	Eliminate costs and create data that provides insight into cost structure and process flows.
Collaboration and Unified Communications Technology	Connect the virtual organization, so that people can drive innovation, maintain relationships, and execute on operational improvements that result in improved productivity. Unified communications create a single communication infrastructure, reducing costs for PBX enhancements while providing information workers with improved productivity through unified inboxes and rules that help them manage interruptions.

Technology	Business Rationale
Security for the Extended Enterprise	As the edges of business and consumer applications blur, security technology will emerge to keep intellectual property and trade secrets secure and to keep personal information about employees and customers confidential.
Virtualization	Virtualization reduces costs for hardware, improves software testing and deployment, reduces energy and physical space use, and increases the flexibility of hardware investments.
Managed Mobility	From e-mail to data on micro-SD cards, enterprise information now resides on company-owned and personal cellular phones. Managed mobility pushes data governance policies out to the edge of the network without significantly affecting the performance of the devices for telephony or collaboration.
Document Management Systems	Centralized repositories of content eliminate multiple versions of the truth and misunderstandings about the "source of truth."
Business Intelligence and Analytics	Having the infrastructure in place to understand business performance, processes, customers, markets, and employees is essential to gaining insights from data.
Business Performance Infrastructure	Adopting a platform through which collaboration, communications, analytics, and enterprise systems all communicate creates a more integrated, responsive, and agile business.

NOTES

1. Carr, N. *Does IT Matter? Information Technology and the Corrosion of Competitive Advantage*. Boston, MA: Harvard Business School Publishing, 2004.
2. Brynjolfsson, Erik. "VII Pillars of Productivity." *Optimize*. May 2005. http://ebusiness.mit.edu/erik/Seven%20Pillars%20of%20Productivity.pdf
3. Bludon, William. "How to Make CRM Work." *Computerworld*. April 11, 2003. http://www.computerworld.com/softwaretopics/crm/story/0,10801,80251,00.html
4. McDowell, Robert and Simon, W. *In Search of Business Value: Ensuring a Return on Your Technology Investment*. New York, NY: SelectBooks Inc., 2004.
5. Hegel, John and Seely Brown, J. "Letter." *Harvard Business Review*, June 2003.

CHAPTER 6

From the New World of Business to the New World of Work

The challenges and opportunities of doing business in the next decade take place against the backdrop of a dynamic, interconnected world. This chapter looks at the social, political, economic, and demographic factors that define the environment in which organizations operate, and delineate the range of uncertainties that decision makers may have to account for in their strategic planning. Because these observations are drawn from our earlier explorations of future scenarios and driving trends, there is some overlap between the material presented here and that in the previous four chapters. The difference is that the New World of Work covers the implications of these driving forces from the perspective of individual workers and managers, in addition to offering strategic priorities for organizations as a whole to consider.

We have chosen to organize the discussion around four key themes shaping the future of work: the impact of globalization; the effect of ubiquitous networks and connectivity; the drive toward transparency; and the evolution of the workforce. Each theme rests on a foundation of data—demographic change in the workforce; increasing efforts by companies, governments, consumers, and citizens to disclose (or protect) information; the rapid spread of connectivity and devices; and the move towards global political and economic integration as manifested by trade negotiations, corporate consolidation, and the increasing interconnectedness of media.

The themes of the new world of work inform the experience of people at a practical level. How might the concept of the workday and the workplace change in light of new and better ways to collaborate across time and distance, and what aspects of work (such as compensation and management) might have to be reconsidered in light of those changes? What challenges does the new landscape of global integration pose for managers and workers? How can organizations best balance the demands for greater transparency and collaboration among partners, while still protecting sensitive data and complying with more stringent government regulations?

These uncertainties about the future of the work experience intersect with issues of business strategy at one crucial point: people. Because the turbulent future of business is so dependent on human knowledge, insight, and leadership, questions about the way we will live and work become crucially important to the decisions organizations must make about management and technology.

ONE WORLD OF BUSINESS

Author Thomas Friedman dates the "flattening of the world" from the fall of the Berlin Wall in 1989, symbolizing the demise of militant international opposition to neoliberal capitalism.[1] At the same time, high-speed networks capable of carrying unprecedented volumes of data effortlessly and instantaneously across vast distances began crisscrossing the world. Information and Communication Technology (ICT) reached "escape velocity" at the exact moment when political barriers dissolved. Since then, the two forces have worked in tandem to bring more of the world's markets and people into a single unified field of communication, information, and commerce.

The intertwined economics of today's world make increasing globalization seem like a sure bet. The incentives for free movement of capital, goods, intellectual property (IP), and labor across borders would seem to be stronger than the inertia of isolationism.[2]

However, both technological innovation and globalization have engendered political opposition from threatened constituencies. Some of the backlash has been disruptive; some has been violent. In some cases, it has caused a necessary reevaluation of the consequences of exposing fragile economies and traditional cultures to the gale-force winds of global change. Does globalism necessarily maintain its momentum in the face of national or religious opposition, or strong economic and environmental objections?[3] The recent collapse of the Doha Round of trade liberalization talks is one indication that political will may be flagging.

While the future of globalism as a political issue may be an open question, businesses today continue to invest as though Friedman's flat world were a permanent feature of the world economy. That means dealing with both the obvious implications (supply chains, costs of entering new markets, mergers and acquisitions, scaling up) and the ones that are not so obvious, such as where new ideas and new competitors might come from in a world that no longer obeys the old rules of geography and local cultures.

Spotting and Nurturing Innovation

One consequence of the flattening of the world is that the locus of innovation is becoming more diffuse. In the past, one place would get "hot" as a result of a concentration of talent, ideas, and capital. Now, technology and easy access to information are allowing innovation to occur independent of physical place.[4] Tracking innovation is no longer a task that requires an organization to focus only on one place. Rather, it is a task that requires the recognition of patterns across a globe dotted by centers of innovation and of individual contributors sharing their insights and evangelizing their ideas from every corner of the globe.

Time is condensing along with space. Cycles of innovation are shortening. New ideas are getting exposed and analyzed by more people, leading to rapid cycles of refinement and rapid discovery and exploitation of weaknesses. One instance where this had a visibly dramatic effect was in the global response to the outbreak of SARS in 2003. Medical authorities in Ontario, Canada (ground zero of the epidemic in North America) reported that, "During the SARS outbreak, Internet resources were called into play for nearly every aspect of disease control, from investigation, surveillance and research, to communication and education."[5] The speed of response was critical in spreading the knowledge necessary to contain the disease. The globalization of knowledge—and the ICT infrastructure that enables it—averted a large-scale public health disaster.

Businesses that can internalize the new rhythms of an interconnected world stand to benefit from more rapid innovation, better access to talent and expertise, and enhanced ability to respond effectively to customers, regulators, partners, and markets. Adaptation requires the right mix of investments to fend off threats while simultaneously and constantly reinventing and innovating to meet the demands of customers and markets.

Capitalizing on Scale

One feature of the integrated global economy is that it provides multiple ways for organizations to take advantage of the benefits of scale, including efficient utilization (and reuse) of resources, reduced costs of entry into new markets, and brand strength.

Many organizations have opted for the traditional method of scaling up—through mergers and acquisitions (M&A). According to McKinsey Consulting, levels of global M&A activity surpassed $4 trillion in 2006, eclipsing the previous peak of $3.3 trillion in 2000.[6] Thomson Financial reports that the value of European technology mergers and acquisitions has more than doubled in the last year, reaching a year-to-date value of $36.4 billion in 2007, compared with $14.4 billion at the same point in 2006.[7]

As organizations scramble to add new capabilities through M&A deals, integrating those capabilities for business value is the next challenge. It requires not only bringing different cultures and groups of people into alignment, but also rationalizing IT assets into a strategy that supports the goals of the combined organization moving forward. Many of these capabilities are available today in products that support a dynamic, optimized business productivity infrastructure. Future innovations will automate many of the tasks associated with integrating database formats, negotiating platform compatibility, resolving security permissions between platforms, and improving search for both people and data.

Cocreating Value with Global Partners

Another way organizations can capitalize on the benefits of scale is through formal partnerships or informal networks for sharing knowledge and capabilities opportunistically. Microsoft, for example, develops core software products, but depends on a network of partners with specialized industry, domain, and geographic expertise to provide customization, localization, and integration. Microsoft collaborates closely with partners by sharing code and knowledge in addition to offering training, support, joint marketing, and other resources. Many partners enjoy access to Microsoft systems and resources and can participate in appropriate activities as though they were formal employees of the company. This leads to more efficient knowledge transfer and more rapid innovation. Customers get all of the benefits of Microsoft's global scale and resources—research and development (R&D) investment, commitment to innovation, ongoing product support and maintenance, among other things—combined with the choice and flexibility of dealing with local partners with specialized knowledge of their business.

Meeting Rising Global Expectations

In at least one aspect, the Web is a victim of its own success. Because so much information is so readily available, and there are so many open forums for knowledge sharing and collaboration, people's expectations have been set to "collaborate" by default. When organizations fail to live up to those expectations because internal policies or old practices make them reluctant to share data or accept input from customers and partners, they can be perceived as unresponsive or difficult to work with. The costs of bearing that reputation in a competitive market must therefore be factored against any perceived benefits of holding information close to the chest.

Balancing Global Collaboration and Security

Until recently, IT has been put in a reactive position in this conversation, promoting restrictive blanket policies to hold the line against worst-case scenarios rather than providing the case-by-case discretion that is increasingly necessary in a complex world. Network-level security (fire-walls, virus protection, anti-spam filters) has long been the first (and sometimes only) line of defense for proprietary data. But as expectations of greater collaboration integration continue to rise, organizations find themselves punching more holes in their perimeter fence to permit access. Sometimes the need for security requires organizations to draw the line farther out than it needs to be, keeping otherwise useful information and practices private because they may contain small elements of proprietary IP that could be compromised. Content-level security, discussed previously, offers a flexible option for organizations to maintain control of documents and data while extending collaboration well beyond the firewall. As content-based security supplants today's need for network-level fences and firewalls, organizations will be able to redirect IT resources toward capabilities that have positive benefits for the business rather than defensive risk management. With the ability to exert precise control over what information and practices to share, businesses can safely share more with customers, partners, government agencies, and others, building greater trust through richer and more routine collaboration.

Differentiating Global Brands with Personalized Service

Customers often encounter friction between brand promises and company performance in the area of customer service. This arises from the inevitable tension between the customer's expectation of being treated as a special individual, and the standardized nature of many customer relationship management (CRM) processes. As companies reach out to broader, more diverse markets across the globe, these tensions are liable to become even more pronounced.

The costs of providing fully individualized service (within brand guidelines) can be prohibitive as the business scales. Some degree of standardized practice is both necessary and desirable. At the same time, even sophisticated, structured CRM processes are prone to encounter exceptions, where the service provider is required to depart from the scripted workflow process and either escalate or resolve the issue on their own initiative. If the service provider does not have the right tools and training at their disposal to deliver satisfaction at that "moment of truth," the likely outcome is customer frustration that threatens the transaction and weakens trust in the brand.[8]

The choice for businesses becomes where to invest—more powerful systems or more empowered workers? Infrastructure and practices may seem to represent a smaller investment than labor costs and training. Companies in developed economies have, therefore, used the openness of globalization to outsource or offshore customer service functions to lower labor-cost markets, using networks to extend the structured workflow practices of the client company to radically disempowered workers. While this has initially succeeded in reducing costs in many cases, it is unlikely to be a sustainable model in the long term for a number of reasons.

Empowering People to Bring the Global Brand to Life

More powerful information worker tools can provide deeper capabilities for workers to deliver on brand promises and meet service expectations on their own initiative. Self-service environments that allow workers to create and provision collaborative team sites, create custom views of data pulled from line-of-business systems, and design supplemental workflow processes using flexible XML-based forms, put the tools for business resilience where the business happens—at the point of contact with the customer. Businesses that provide information workers with flexible tools and latitude to apply their insights and talents can result in higher valued interactions and improved productivity when compared to businesses that concentrate only on process.

Operating Effectively in a Diverse World

Organizations that do business on a global scale inevitably encounter the inherent complexity of diversity. Not only market conditions, but social and political norms, expectations, and modes of communication still vary considerably from place to place. Critics of globalization fear that one of its effects will be the homogenization of world culture. Perhaps. But the liquidation of cultural distinctiveness is neither inevitable nor desirable. Globalization does not necessarily imply homogeneity beyond common processes and protocols, so successful businesses will need to factor in inherent diversity of the world as they plan global strategies. Global organizations would be better served by adapting to the complexities of local tastes and practices, finding ways to adopt and incorporate local market needs into their delivery of goods and services, and seeking diversity as a source of novel ideas, innovative styles, and unique modes of expression.

Although it will require a careful balance of global goals and local needs, a new generation of information technology can help organizations harness complexity as a way to remain adaptive and to turn adaptation into innovation. Overlaying more technology without consideration of its impact on already overwhelmed information workers could aggravate rather than alleviate the very problems of complexity that it is intended to address.

Thriving in a Global Economy

Collaboration, responsiveness, and innovation are the three determinants for business success in the New World of Work. In each case, the ability of businesses to respond to the challenges depends on giving people the power and flexibility to act decisively. That means reducing the weight of technology and structured processes on information work by making those processes more seamless and more abstract.

The business challenges of a global, interconnected world demand human insight and human action—supported by information and technology, but not determined by them. Empowering information workers with powerful tools to collaborate, participate, and innovate in the context of their familiar tasks gives organizations the resiliency they will need to adapt, and perhaps even anticipate, the reality of constant change that characterizes our new global economy.

ALWAYS ON, ALWAYS CONNECTED

Access to information from a wide variety of systems, across a plethora of networks, has created new challenges for information workers while seemingly solving some basic information and connectivity needs. People today are distracted not just by meetings, phone calls, and drop-ins by colleagues, but by e-mail, instant messaging, unsatisfying search engine results, and invitations to join or participate in social networks. The increase in connectivity makes it harder for people to draw lines between their work and their personal lives. The mere existence of pervasive connectivity creates expectations that people will make themselves available for work or communication at all hours—expectations that can add considerably to the stress of both work and life. It challenges employers to seek new models that recognize that work no longer has boundaries and that workers are drawing new ones themselves.

Connecting with Better Tools

The new requirements of the connected world are best met with evolving information work tools and practices that build on the knowledge and comfort people already have with the tools they use for working independently. Emerging technology can help people better manage their exposure to the various channels of communications, make working from home or on the road seamless and productive, and simplify the synchronization of data between networks and devices.

New information work technologies can also help organizations achieve the long-promised benefits of virtualization and decentralization. Businesses will be able to adopt business models that include a global workforce that can be managed irrespective of physical location, giving remote, mobile, and temporary workers the access to information resources—and the same management oversight and expectations—experienced by workers operating under more traditional arrangements. People will have far greater opportunities to balance work and life priorities while regaining time lost to commuting and unproductive communication tasks. This, in turn, will allow them to focus on the tasks that will help them accomplish their goals and those of their organizations.

Accommodating the Distributed Workstyles of Digital Natives

Millennials have lived their entire lives in the digital, connected world. Cell phones, networked video games, instant messaging, chat rooms, and other forms of distance communication are not novelties to these people but part of their expectations of work and life. Their experiences and outlook may make them more likely to embrace the flexibility and opportunities of workforce decentralization. The popularity of consumer-based social and collaborative services such as Facebook, MySpace, and Twitter means that many Millennials will arrive in the workforce with considerable familiarity with collaborative tools and practices, and will expect these facilities from their employer.

Enabling Work/Life Balance

As Millennials and their slightly older peers begin starting their own families, the familiar issues of childcare and its impact on workforce productivity (and participation) come into play. According to a U.S. Department of Labor study, "An estimated 10 to 20 percent of nonworking mothers with young children do not seek employment because childcare is not available or affordable. In addition, about 20 to 25 percent of employed mothers would work longer hours if they did not have childcare constraints."[9] Another study found that 37 percent of highly qualified women and 43 percent of women with children leave the workforce for a period of time. Ninety-three percent of those women said they want to return to their careers, but only 74 percent managed to do so. An even more disturbing statistic for employers: Only 5 percent of highly qualified women looking to return to work want to rejoin the company they left. That number drops to zero in business sectors. The study speculates that the reason for this finding is that many women felt underappreciated by their employers when they left their jobs.[10]

At the other end of the demographic scale, increasing numbers of Baby Boomers will opt to remain in the workforce past traditional retirement age, out of either preference or economic necessity. As improvements in healthcare increase the age of the population in general, a growing number of workers will be faced with the costs and time commitments of caring for elderly parents in their eighties and nineties or attending to their own health and wellness. Forty-four million Americans engage in the care of an older loved one. Fifteen to 25 percent of the workforce now care for older or disabled loved ones, and by 2010, the percentage is expected to double. Family caregivers struggle to balance their work and elder-care obligations. This juggling act often affects a worker's health, finances, and family and social life—and it results in lost productivity at work.[11]

Technology solutions such as remote and mobile access can make it easier for working families to be high-value contributors by allowing them to stay connected to the people, processes, and information of the workplace even when they are not there. Investments in collaboration and communications technologies will help unlock personal and economic potential for people, employers, and communities as the new realities of the work world evolve.

Rethinking Management in the Always On, Always Connected World

The virtualization of information work will require a radical rethinking of long-held assumptions about the distinction between work and private life, modes of compensation, employee measurement systems,[12] relevant job skills, the supervisory role of management, and the nature of place.[13] Employers and workers should be prepared to open discussions around:

- *Task-based compensation.* Because physical attendance at a workplace will not be required for many information work jobs, many workers will be measured and compensated on a task or project basis rather than with hourly wages.[14] In addition, some organizations will adopt a more flexible commitment-based employee measurement system that allows the employee to better choose how, where, and when he or she works, while fitting into an overall set of dates and commitments.[15]

- *Negotiated boundaries.* Ubiquitous access to work processes and information will no longer be a technical challenge or a competitive differentiator for businesses and people, but rather a background assumption in the negotiations between the firm and its workers about how, when, and where work is performed. Employers may find the ability to offer flexible work arrangements a competitive advantage in attracting top talent.

- *New job skills.* People who are able to effectively manage their time and attention while working independently, without direct supervision, will have a competitive advantage in virtualized roles. It is likely that a secondary industry of training and support for virtual workers will emerge,[16] in addition to a strong demand for home-office and community-office design and supply.[17]

- *New management practices.* Driving high levels of productivity and innovation from virtual teams and decentralized organizations is uncharted territory for many traditional managers. Indeed, many experiments in outsourcing and offshoring end up generating significantly higher costs (or lower savings) than anticipated because of difficulties in managing teams by remote control.[18] Very soon, however, a body of best practices will begin to emerge. The sooner organizations and managers can adopt and internalize the skills needed to thrive in a virtualized environment, the sooner they will realize the significant economic, social, and environmental benefits that decentralization makes possible.

Dealing with Information Overload

Information overload is already a measurable productivity-killer. In 2005, HP and the University of London conducted a study on the impact of constant interruptions on human intelligence. They came to the colorful and oft-quoted conclusion that a distracted worker's effective IQ drops nearly 10 points—twice the average drop caused by using marijuana.[19] HP and the University of London went so far as to develop a handbook for avoiding "info-mania," whose abstract reads:

> The abuse of 'always-on' technology has led to a nationwide state of Info-Mania where UK workers are literally addicted to checking e-mail and text messages during meetings, in the evening and at weekends. Mobile technology offers massive productivity benefits when used responsibly, but inappropriate use can be negative.[20]

The problem here isn't necessarily the ubiquity of access, but people's inability to manage it effectively. As communication and identity management become more integrated across networks, systems, and devices, unified presence management will be important to regulating a person's exposure to interruptions, communication, processes, and information. Users will be able to control who can reach them, at what hours, on what device(s), using what channels (voice, instant message, e-mail, fax, and other devices). Senders will know whether to expect a real-time conversation, a return call, or a return message based on the recipient's reported presence status.

Making Information Useful

Managers spend two hours a day looking for information they need, and almost half the data is useless once they get it, according to a study by Accenture of 1,009 managers at U.S.- and U.K.-based companies, reported by *InformationWeek*.[21]

New technologies can provide better context for information so that ubiquity of access translates effectively into business value. The increasing use of metadata to describe content stored in data repositories can provide a more flexible, adaptive way to associate documents, people, and records with relevant search terms, without having to maintain cumbersome taxonomies. This "smart content" will update its metadata description each time it is used and accessed, and it will dynamically update references to all documents that cite or include it. When combined with adaptive filtering and pattern recognition capabilities of next-generation search engines and security/identity protocols, content and documents will be at once more accessible and more secure.

This way, a distributed business can rest firmly on a single information management platform. Employees, partners, customers, and other interested parties will have comprehensive access to relevant data, with access privileges automatically determined by their role, task, and level of permissions.

Staying Connected in an Always On World

People and organizations need to prepare for dramatic changes brought about by ubiquitous connectivity. Those who are drawn into the always-on, always-connected world without adequate investment in the right technology and practices risk enormous problems in sustaining productivity, morale, and overall competitiveness. "Information overload" and the anxieties associated with constant exposure to communication are real, and they rapidly reach a point of diminishing returns.

Conversely, organizations and people who use and manage connectivity to their advantage will enjoy a number of benefits. People will have greater freedom, greater control of their time, and greater flexibility to balance work and life commitments. Organizations will be able to sustain productivity and extend their operations and culture worldwide with enhanced management control and visibility because communications and collaboration technology will give them even better connections to their global workforce than they experience with a geographically concentrated workforce.

TRANSPARENT ORGANIZATIONS

Transparency in a business context is sometimes seen as a euphemism for compliance. That is, disclosures are motivated by statute, by labor agreement, or by some special relationship between a company and its partners or customers. Over the past few years, however, at least as much pressure for transparency has been coming from the bottom up as from the top down. This dynamic is turning the old business logic on its head: Transparency is no longer just the law; it's also a good idea.

The easy availability of information on the Web, whether from traditional "authoritative" sources or from the growing store of reliable user-created content on blogs, social networks, wikis, and communities, creates the expectations that everything, sooner or later, will get out in the open. It also creates the perception that privacy is no longer the default (e.g., people are anonymous unless they choose not to be), but is instead something fragile that requires the active intervention of government or some affirmative declaration of social responsibility on the part of a company with respect to its data.

There are several indications that transparency is likely to be a durable and defining theme for the new world of work. First, keeping secrets is increasingly difficult and costly, and the consequences of withholding information for self-serving or arbitrary reasons can be instantaneous and severe. Second, it pays to be open. Transparency actually improves processes like innovation, customer service, and partner relationships because people generally prefer to be included in conversations and have some visibility into processes. When organizations or employers extend trust, they are repaid with loyalty, productivity, and good ideas. Third, the economic climate as we approach the end of 2008 has exposed the systemic failures of opacity—particularly in the financial markets, but also in areas such as consumer product safety—and this is likely to fuel public demand for increased regulation of businesses, either by legislation or by other mechanisms.

Adapting to a More Transparent Workplace

IT systems have been driving transparency in the workplace for decades, by giving business managers insights the inputs and outputs of structured processes such as operations, sales, supply chain, and finance. Now, knowledge-sharing and collaboration systems are extending that transparency to ordinary information work tasks. Documents that were once stored away in file cabinets or on individual PCs are now visible in enterprise data repositories. Expertise location systems are making it easier to find people, even when their expertise and experience is not reflected in their job title. Now social computing applications on the consumer Web and in the enterprise are exposing tacit knowledge and facilitating millions of informal conversations and exchanges of information.

The net result is that information workers talk more, and are talked about more, than ever before. Job applicants have information about potential employers and the compensation packages that competitors are offering before they walk in the door, even as interviewers are looking up their old MySpace sites for some clues to their outside lives. Workers can disclose damaging information on blogs and social networks if they are disgruntled—or reach out to their personal network to solve a work-related problem faster than any support desk. Customers can complain loudly in public if they do not receive the service they expect—or become the most credible ambassadors for your brand, with value far in excess of the best PR that any agency could deliver, if you can satisfy them.

Reducing the Cost and Complexity of Compliance

The U.S. government responded to the corporate scandals of the late 1990s with the Sarbanes-Oxley Act (SOX), mandating tighter guidelines for disclosure of financial data and making chief executives personally legally responsible for the veracity of their corporation's reported results.[22] Companies also must track and retain communication and transaction data according to complex and specific requirements and be able to produce that data in reports. Other governments either already have or are contemplating similar regulations.

The economic dilemma is that the benefits accrue to the market system as a whole, but the compliance and governance costs fall on individual firms. Technology is a key component of those costs, accounting for a projected average increase of 10 to 15 percent in IT costs to U.S.

companies in 2006, according to a Gartner Inc., study.[23] From an IT perspective, there is no ROI on compliance as such; there are just penalties for noncompliance. As a result, many organizations see investments in compliance as costs with few benefits. It is not strategic. It is just compliance, and there are incentives to deploy the lowest cost solution that meets current requirements.

SOX and its European counterpart, Basel II, are not the only compliance challenges facing organizations. There are over 700 state and federal privacy compliance laws that companies are required to navigate, including newly added compliance laws in the United States,[24] such as the Federal Rules of Civil Procedure (FRCP), which went into effect at the beginning of 2007. FRCP compliance regulations require companies to know where all electronic records are stored, including corporate e-mail, to make them available to courts in the case of a lawsuit. According to a summary of a recent study done in late February 2007 by Fortiva, almost two months after this new regulation went into effect, 94 percent of those responsible for e-mail policy do not feel their organization is completely prepared to meet FRCP requirements, only 38 percent of the respondents said they were familiar with the changes, and 45 percent of the respondents reported they have no retention policy.[25] The study reports that, "up to 70 percent of business data resides in e-mail ... [and] e-mail is now just as likely to be requested during legal discovery as are paper-based records. More than 60 percent of organizations have been ordered by a court or regulatory body to produce corporate e-mail."[26]

Making Compliance Less Burdensome on Information Workers

Market transparency and compliance capabilities should be organic to the environment of information worker productivity and to the platform, not a patch to existing systems or a stand-alone solution with its own usage and governance issues. The advantages of building compliance capabilities into the information work application environment are to make it relatively easy for people to change the business rules for transaction monitoring, reporting, and retention without reworking the entire technology framework and without the extensive participation of IT. This makes organizations far more resilient to changing regulatory environments and reduces the cost of operating in multiple regulatory jurisdictions with inconsistent requirements.

Applying Transparency for Better Internal Controls

Transparency is often driven by compliance requirements, but its benefits do not end there. Decision makers can use visibility into operational practices at a granular level to make continual improvements. More powerful networked systems for information work can provide metrics and metadata to give executives richer insights into areas such as structured tasks and exception handling, project management, document management, CRM and hard-to-quantify activities such as teamwork.

Likewise, people can be more productive when they understand how their work aligns with larger business objectives. Systems that allow workers to visualize social networks, publish, and subscribe to unstructured communication channels (such as blogs and discussion groups), and identify and propagate best practices in their own areas of expertise can enhance personal and organizational productivity.

Fostering Open Participation

Open participation through new workplace-based social networking technologies such as employee portals, communities of practice (where experts within or across organizations can exchange ideas informally in threaded news, e-mail, and discussion groups), blogs (self-published, often informally organized Web pages expressing personal and professional insights of the author), and expertise location services (search engines that discover personal contact information of document authors and experts along with the documents themselves) can lead to rapid and exciting breakthroughs based on pooled knowledge and experience of the people closest to the business processes. Don Tapscott and David Ticoll, in *The Naked Corporation: How the Age of Transparency Will Revolutionize Business,* identify a number of areas where openness as a cultural value can promote greater identification of employees with organizational objectives, better worker morale, and improved information for decision-makers as a result of workers being more willing to be candid and honest in communications with peers and managers.[27]

Unfortunately, these benefits are notoriously difficult to quantify. In addition, firms run the risk that too much knowledge-sharing in the name of transparency generates more heat than light, distracting employees from their specific focus without establishing a reliable process for the creation of new value. In some organizations, empowering a bottom-up transparency model is a zero-sum game at the expense of management control. Many traditionally hierarchical organizations may not find the benefits of transparency to be worth the cultural costs. Finally, there is the question of legitimate confidentiality and IP protection. Some information is not appropriate to share, either within or outside an organization. Even the most permissively transparent organization must and should have its opaque areas and the means to strictly limit and monitor the distribution of private information.

Bringing Transparency to Structured Work Tasks

Structured information work in areas such as call centers, help desks, order taking, project management, and some types of product and document development are much easier to quantify and make transparent. Often the systems that support structured information work include capabilities for sophisticated measurement of worker practices. However, if these systems are proprietary, it can be difficult to expose the data necessary to generate a cross-enterprise strategic view of overall productivity across processes and systems.

Web services architectures (WSAs) are beginning to solve this problem. WSAs expose data from different systems in a common schema, where they can be presented to end users in a single interface—either in a portal or through a front-end application such as spreadsheet software like Microsoft Excel. This information can be presented to decision-makers in a consistent format, such as an electronic form, executive scorecard, or digital dashboard to provide real-time, at-a-glance data about enterprise performance. Executives can then use visually oriented workflow design and management tools to make high-level adjustments to workflow and business rules, while the application negotiates the back-end system modifications automatically.

New visualization technologies will provide managers and executives with better tools with which to see into processes. Vivid, large-scale displays can present visual information with greater clarity and resolution. Faster processors and distributed computing enable the rendering of abstract organizational models as interactive multidimensional objects that users can examine and manipulate. This mode of interacting with complex data in real time will be second nature to a generation of information workers raised on increasingly sophisticated video games and simulations.

Balancing Privacy and Productivity

The principle drawback is that many workers, particularly information workers, are resistant to what they see as "big brotherism" in the workplace—unless their expectations are set ahead of time and they embrace the business justification for the collection of information. Surreptitious or unduly intrusive monitoring can have a markedly detrimental effect on workplace morale and corporate culture, and it can engender feelings of hostility among workers that can rebound strongly against employers. The more that authority and discretion are traditionally associated with the information work role, the more likely a negative reaction becomes and the more resources are available to the worker for effective retaliation (that is, whistleblowing or disclosure of organizational "dirty laundry" on Web sites).

Regulatory compliance can help reduce this friction because it sets expectations that the employer will collect and use certain employee data out of legal obligation, not simply management's desire for control. Knowing that their employers must monitor certain data, workers adjust their behavior accordingly.[28]

Increasing the Transparency of Partnerships and Supply Networks

For organizations dependent on just-in-time relationships with downstream vendors of parts and services, providing transparency into the specific processes enables partners to proactively anticipate demand, adjust their own processes, and reduce costly lags, friction, and uncertainty. Many businesses already provide extranets and application-level integration to partners to assist with forecasting, order-tracking, billing, information-sharing, and person-to-person communication.

Often, however, these systems do not provide the full measure of transparency and value because of concerns over proprietary IP and system security. Sometimes the integration of heterogeneous systems entails costs and complexities greater than the immediate benefits. Sometimes corporate culture is resistant to partnership or keeps distance in business relationships through restricted access to outsiders. Technological innovation can help reduce many of these barriers to formal and informal collaboration with partners by giving organizations more precise ways to manage the level of transparency they permit to partners, increasing not only the comfort levels for partners but their willingness to participate as well.

Building Trust Through Reputation

Customers increasingly want more than basic transactions: They want a relationship with a trusted vendor. This element of trust is especially important in a venue such as the Internet, where face-to-face contact is rare and many suppliers have weak to nonexistent brands.

Companies such as eBay, and Amazon.com, have developed ingenious methods for investing trust in otherwise anonymous online transactions. Others, such as Angie's List and Yelp, are using the scale and reach of the Internet to drive greater customer visibility into previously-opaque local markets for small business services. The credibility of these kinds of systems comes from their absolute transparency and bottom-up quality. Users trust each other in the aggregate more than they trust any single partner individually. Good traders, good books, good contractors, and best practices get rapid and broad exposure; bad actors are quickly singled out and avoided by the larger community before they can damage the integrity of the system.

Doing Business in the Fishbowl of Consumer Vigilance

As corporations and large organizations assume a greater influence in the day-to-day lives of people around the world, many people want ways to hold them accountable. Today, new technologies are affording consumers unprecedented access to information about businesses to motivate their actions, and rapid, powerful ways to coordinate their actions, on a global scale if need be. Tools such as social networks, blogs, chat rooms, and reputation systems that rank companies according to criteria of interest to specific customer groups help consumers and advocacy organizations level the playing field with corporate marketing departments by rapidly propagating news, impressions, and information through vast, and largely trusted, channels.

Used effectively and responsibly, "netroots" campaigns can create enormous pressures for accountability and have already forced corporations to respond to unexpected challenges. In November 2005, Sony was forced to withdraw a digital rights management application it had secretly embedded in some of its commercial CDs that installed itself on customers' computers, sometimes causing unexpected problems. A single user posting on a technical blog site identified the problem,[29] traced it back to the Sony CD, and ignited a firestorm of consumer resentment almost overnight. As irate customers were joined by popular recording artists unwilling to publicly support Sony's strategy, the company made a series of withdrawals before finally capitulating entirely on an issue it had seen as central to its ability to protect its revenue streams from IP assets.[30]

The lesson here is that businesses operating in an immediately transparent environment will need to be far more open and responsive to customers on a range of issues to win the trust necessary for a successful brand. The alternative—counting on secrecy and public inattention—is unlikely to be as effective as it was in the past.

From an information work perspective, workers and management will need to consider the implications of even straightforward decisions from the perspective of public impact and customer opinion. In an atmosphere where internal communications and confidential documents could become suddenly and embarrassingly public, organizations need to internalize values of honesty and responsiveness. Strategies such as preemptive disclosure, ombudsmen and internal customer advocates, corporate citizenship initiatives, and a general default stance toward transparency can go a long way to reduce friction between commercial players, their customers, and their communities.

WORKFORCE EVOLUTION

The workforce is evolving through demographic transition and through the changing nature of work. This is challenging workers and organizations to re-think the way they approach a range of workforce issues across the whole lifecycle of employment: education and training, recruitment and retention, compensation and the structure of employment, work/life balance, succession planning, and retirement. Despite the clarity of demographic data, the resolution of these questions remains profoundly uncertain. The next 10–15 years will likely feature a lot of experimentation (and consequently a lot of failure), as people and organizations struggle to accommodate different workstyles, different priorities, and different skill-sets while remaining competitive in a global economy characterized by increasing skills shortages and difficult political choices.

Facing the Skills Gap

The baby boom that followed the end of World War II in most Western countries provided a plentiful supply of young people, who availed themselves of the best education and economic opportunities in history and developed into a formidable army of talent that powered the workforce for nearly 40 years. Now, the leading edge of the Baby Boom generation (born 1946–1962) is poised at the edge of traditional retirement age. According to U.S. Census reports, 7,918 Americans turned 60 every day in 2006, which amounts to 330 every hour[31] —a rate that will only accelerate in the next 10 years. The cohort that follows the baby boom is far smaller, at less than 53 million in the United States (fewer in Europe), compared to over 78 million American Baby Boomers. The 80-million strong Millennial Generation (born 1981–2000) is increasingly asserting itself in the workplace, the consumer market, and in society, but will not be fully vested in the workforce until well into the second decade of the 21st century.

As a result, organizations of all sizes and in all industries around the world are facing a near-term shortage in skilled workers, just at the moment when technology is becoming far more sophisticated and central to critical business processes. The skills shortage means that employers will need to cast a wider net to find the workers they need. Organizations will look to immigrants, overseas workers, older people, and those from more diverse educational and economic backgrounds to supplement the traditional workforce. They will also compete fiercely for the services of younger workers, whose values, expectations, and work styles may be at odds with existing organizational cultures.

Managing Digital Natives

Where will employers find workers to fill necessary positions? Younger workers are one obvious answer, but attracting, motivating and retaining next-generation talent in 2010 requires a different approach than it did in 1970 or 1990. The Millennial Generation has grown up surrounded by digital, interactive media—video games, the Internet, instant messaging, and a cornucopia of entertainment options. As educator Marc Prensky calculates, a typical 21-year-old entering the workforce today has, on average, played 5,000 hours of video games, exchanged 250,000 e-mails, instant messages, and phone text messages, and spent 10,000 hours on a mobile phone in addition to spending 3,500 hours online.[32] Their perceptions are therefore shaped to a large degree by these experiences, which they will carry with them into the workplace.

Sociologists who have studied the emerging generation identify some characteristics common across Millennials from different regional, economic, and ethnic backgrounds. These include:

- Special: feeling of being vital to the nation and to their parents' sense of purpose
- Sheltered: kid safety rules, lockdown of public schools, sweeping national youth safety movement
- Confident: high levels of trust and optimism
- Team Oriented: classroom emphasis on group learning, school uniforms, tighter peer bonds
- Achieving: accountability and higher school standards
- Pressured: to excel in many different areas
- Conventional: social rules can help; comfortable with parents' values[33]

They will likely demonstrate technological sophistication, streetsmarts, a penchant for collaboration, and positive aspirations in the workplace, but Millennials may require greater supervision and positive reinforcement by management than older workers.[34]

Millennials in the workforce will be motivated by the opportunity to work with other bright and creative people, to gain personal recognition for their work, and to make a positive social impact.[35] The values, nurtured upbringing, social conscience, and sophistication of this generation promise to make them extraordinary contributors in the workplace, provided employers take needed steps to accommodate their unique needs and expectations.

They also have higher expectations with respect to technology. For the most talented and productive new workers, constant access to information and colleagues is a baseline assumption. Organizations can harness the enthusiasm and fresh thinking of younger workers by making investments in ICT systems and practices that align with their high level of skills and expectations.

Perhaps most importantly, Millennials have a set of social expectations that translate into a lower need to strive toward higher responsibility at work and a willingness to give up some level of pay and benefits to retain a more flexible, socially oriented lifestyle. This will result in high turnover rates for Millennials. This trend, combined with the aging of the baby-boom generation, will create a high need for organizations to manage the intellectual assets of their workforce so they can quickly bring in new talent, learn from that talent, and capture that knowledge before they depart—at the same time capturing important knowledge from their older workers that will need to be transferred to new workers in new ways, as long-term mentoring is unlikely to be a model over the next several decades.[36]

Maximizing the Productivity of "Boomerang Boomers"

It might be that the best person for tomorrow's job may be the person in that job today, even if they are at or near retirement age. A recent AARP/Roper survey indicated that 80 percent of Baby Boomers are planning to work at least part-time during their retirement. Sometimes this is by choice; other times it is driven by financial necessity, as many older workers face inadequate incomes in retirement.[37] Several futurists believe that seniors who defer retirement past the traditional age of 65 may experience longer, healthier lives as a result of the continued challenges and stimulation of work,[38] helping to address some of the issues around wellness and preventative healthcare noted above.

Tapping Into the Global Talent Pool

While globalization and technology are making it possible to bring high-value work to labor markets overseas, the traditional dynamic of workers physically relocating to the site of jobs—migration and immigration—will remain a feature of the New World of Work.

The issue of information-worker immigration is already a controversial one in the United States, whose H-1B visa program provides special (and expedited) "guest worker" status for overseas workers with specialized skills demanded by U.S. employers. Proponents of the H-1B system who favor fewer restrictions and higher quotas for foreign skilled workers claim that the American education system is not producing enough workers with high-level math, science, IT, and engineering skills. H-1B immigration preserves jobs in the domestic economy by enabling employers to fill necessary roles without having to offshore entire project groups or divisions to overseas labor markets. Opponents believe that the influx of skilled workers from lower wage overseas markets depresses wages in the United States and dilutes the negotiating power of American workers.[39]

As emerging economies achieve higher levels of workforce development, the pressure either to bring skilled workers to developed markets through expedited visa programs or to offshore entire information-work projects, divisions, and industries to lower cost markets will grow. Freer immigration gives skilled workers greater choices about where they can work, and it allows them to capitalize fully on both employment and lifestyle opportunities on a global scale. It also provides a solution for employers whose workforce needs are not adequately served by the domestic labor markets. It must be noted, however, that immigration is an issue with social and political dimensions in addition to economic ones. Proponents—employers in particular—should be sensitive to these external considerations when advocating increased opportunities for immigration, and they should balance calls for higher immigration with promises to invest in the development of the domestic workforce to ensure that the benefits of well-paid information-work jobs are equitably distributed.

Looking to New Industries for New Sources of Opportunity

Just as good high-tech and biotech jobs today were unimaginable just a few years ago, new innovations will continue to create entire industries and occupational categories in the years ahead. The May 2005 issue of *Technology Review* profiled several new technologies that will likely lead to new industries, including: airborne networks for aviation, quantum wires for energy, silicon photonics in optoelectronics, metabolomics in medicine, magnetic-resonance force microscopy in imaging, bacterial factories in pharmaceuticals, environmatics for the environment, and biomechatronics for improved prosthetics. Each of these heady-sounding technologies will create new supportive information-work roles for their design and maintenance and for broad adoption and deployment. Information work will be a key component in the success of industries to be build around these emerging technologies and around new technologies and business models that have yet to emerge from the level of supposition or experiment.

Adapting to Adaptability

Adaptability is becoming the watchword of a successful workforce as the single-job, single-employer career path of the industrial age recedes into history. Most people working today will face significant changes in the skills, practices, and responsibilities of their jobs over the course of their working life. Many will need to learn new skills and new technologies; some will require retraining across the entire work skill set as their old jobs are no longer economically viable in the face of low-cost offshore labor or automation. Workers who are not just educated but *educable* will find these transitions far less disruptive than those who lack fundamental grounding in knowing how to learn.

The education system bears the burden of preparing workers for this New World of Work. It is a fundamentally different challenge than this system faced even a generation ago, when it was still possible to expect that low-skill industrial work could provide sufficient economic rewards and that a social safety net would catch those who fell through the cracks. But if the mission of education in the information age has changed, its approaches have been slow to adapt.

Technological change is occurring so rapidly that it is hard to predict exactly what specific skills will be required for the highly valued jobs of tomorrow, or what jobs of today may follow the buggy-whip maker and the typesetter into the footnotes of labor history. However, one predictable feature of the current economy is the ability of innovation to bring entire new classes of work into existence to replace those rendered obsolete. Yesterday's displaced steelworker may well have become today's network administrator. Today's call-center worker may, with the right training, go on to play some highly valuable role in a completely new job created by widespread adoption of social-networking technology.

Primary and secondary education needs to provide the solid fundamentals for a lifetime of learning. It is less important for students to learn the specifics of information-work skills and practices than to master the intellectual building blocks necessary to produce and use information. These include math and science, with special emphasis on the scientific method as a discipline for evidence-based discovery and decision-making, communication, and comprehension. As smarter, simpler information-work software buries the complexities of use and process, the value of these highly role-specific skills may decline in relation to more generalized intellectual, analytic, experiential, interpersonal, and creative talents. The ability to find and format information, for example, will be less important because the software provides a higher degree of context and automation for those sorts of tasks. However, the judgment to know which information is the most reliable, how to evaluate risk and reward, how to persuade colleagues and learn from mistakes—these will be the value-add for human information workers.

In addition, education can incorporate new approaches made possible by technology. Future information-work occupations are likely to involve the construction and manipulation of models, both abstract and visual, to help anticipate outcomes based on a complicated set of initial conditions. Schools can use new systems and software that allow students to build and visualize models using rich interactive tools. Many students of the recent generation have already received significant "informal" training in this area from video games and interactive multimedia software. As visualization, modeling, and simulation capabilities become integrated into mainstream information-work applications, schools should find ways to incorporate these practices into the formal curriculum.

Embracing Lifelong Learning

To the extent that these skills rely on the broad values of the humanities, ethics, history, and rhetoric that may be missing from the educational background of many current workers, continuing education programs will need to fill the gaps. According to futurist Peter Drucker, "The fastest-growing industry in any developed country may turn out to be the *continuing education* of already well-educated adults, based on values that are all but incompatible with those of the youth culture." Much of it will be delivered in nontraditional ways and places—in community centers and via distance learning, rather than in classrooms.[40] Government, corporate interests, and nonprofits can support improved life-long learning for disadvantaged youth and adults by providing technology-related skills through community-based technology learning centers. Publicly accessible gathering places represent prime locations where people can go beyond merely having access to technology and can acquire the skills to use technology effectively to help themselves and their communities. A growing number of for-profit education centers will provide specialized and supplementary education for adults and youths, financed by paid tuition or a creative combination of funding from public, private, corporate, and nonprofit sources.[41] Already we see examples of this in the rapid expansion of companies like the University of Phoenix, which has branch campuses in many cities around the United States and elsewhere.

Investing in Social Infrastructure

Attracting innovative businesses and high-value information workers is a major priority for national and local governments because a dense core of innovation can have wide-reaching secondary benefits for the entire regional economy. Many global businesses do not have a strict economic need to be located in major population centers, nor do information workers whose talents are in global demand. Still, even decentralized businesses need a hub from which innovation and management can flow to remote suppliers. Likewise, information workers need to live somewhere, even if they are working at home or in branch offices far from the corporate center. The question of location, which had historically been a matter of economic necessity, is increasingly becoming a matter of choice.

And what drives those choices? According to sociologist Richard Florida, it comes down to lifestyle and social infrastructure. Florida writes of a "creative class" of innovative individuals and entrepreneurs: the elites of the information economy whose ideas and labor generate massive economic value, and spur the vitality of entire regions.[42] And they are drawn to specific cities (even specific neighborhoods) for reasons that have more to do with aesthetics than economic necessity. Florida recommends that localities make investments in social infrastructure—art, culture, recreation facilities, family-friendly surroundings, and tolerant politics—to draw a critical mass of "creative class" talent and benefit from the economic activity that they generate.

Empowering Tomorrow's Workforce

Investing in the empowerment of people offers win-win answers to many of these challenges. It will prepare workers for higher value, higher reward occupations; it will provide businesses with the talent they need to innovate and compete; and it will provide governments with the heightened productivity necessary to promote economic growth and meet transfer payment obligations. These investments include:

- Technology to empower workers, and especially the high-value information workers, whose creativity and ideas lead to the most dramatic innovations.

- Continuing education, to ensure that current and future workers have the skills, context, and judgment to use information effectively to drive economic benefits.

- New education models in K–12, to make sure that students learn at an early age that learning itself is important, and that the ability to adapt to change is as important as the ability to master facts. Curriculums in the future need to feature constructivist learning models that foster collaboration and model the kinds of interpersonal skills that next-generation workers will need to master.

- Cross-generational workplaces, to incorporate the wisdom and experience of older workers along with the new ideas and approaches of the emerging generation, while engaging the productive capabilities of those who choose to continue working.

- Equitable workplaces, where technology and management practices support productive, mutually beneficial collaboration between workers, management, and ownership.
- Workforce mobility and decentralization, where appropriate, to capture the wasted resources consumed by commuting and enable workers and organizations to operate with the flexibility that new conditions demand.
- Strong, vibrant communities, with the physical, educational, environmental, information, and cultural infrastructure to nurture creative, productive, and engaged individuals and families.

Deployed effectively, these investments can make the transition to the more global, interconnected New World of Work smoother and spread the benefits more broadly. They can diffuse the tensions associated with globalization, demographic change, and technological innovation and help push the global economy toward a sustainable era of growth and prosperity.

NOTES

1. Friedman, T. *The World is Flat*. Farrar, Straus and Giroux, 2005.
2. Persuasive discussions can be found in Wolf, M. *Why Globalization Works*. Yale University Press, 2004; and Bhagwati, J. *In Defense of Globalization*. Oxford University Press, 2004, among others.
3. For perspectives on possible antiglobalism scenarios ranging from the skeptical to the catastrophic, see Kelly, K. *Out of Control: The New Biology of Machines, Social Systems and the Economic World*. Perseus, 1995; Barber, B. *Jihad vs. McWorld: How Globalism and Tribalism are Reshaping the World*. Ballantine Books, 1996; and Kunstler, J. H. *The Long Emergency: Surviving the End of the Oil Age, Global Climate Change, and Other Converging Catastrophes of the 21st Century*. Atlantic Books, 2005.
4. See Florida, R. *The Flight of the Creative Class*. Harper Business, 2005, for a thorough analysis of the growing global diffusion of innovation and the changing role of place.
5. "The Role of Technology in the Global Response to SARS." Ontario Medical Association, October 1, 2003. www.oma.org/pcomm/OMR/oct/03ww.htm
6. *McKinsey Quarterly*, December 1, 2006.
7. Reported by Lara Williams, *Computing*, May 23, 2007.www.computing.co.uk/computing/news/2190540/thomson-financial-figures

8. Seddon, J. *Freedom from Command and Control.* Vanguard Education Ltd., 2003. Seddon argues that overly structured systems can have unintended consequences in areas where human discretion can be more effective, such as customer service. He advocates a more system-wide strategic view involving greater worker empowerment, which can benefit workers, managers, and customers alike.

9. Harriet B. Presser and Amy G. Cox. "The Work Schedules of Low-Educated American Women and Welfare Reform." *Monthly Labor Review,* April 1997, p. 26, cited at www.dol.gov/asp/programs/history/herman/reports/ future-work/report/chapter3/main.htm.

10. "Off-Ramps and On-Ramps: Keeping Talented Women on the Road to Success." Conducted by the Center for Work-Life Policy.

11. *Workforce Management* Online, April 2007. According to a study by MetLife Insurance (MetLife Caregiving Cost Study: Productivity Losses to U.S. Business, 2006 www.workforce.com/archive/feature/24/85/10/index.php?ht=), the cost to U.S. business from the lost productivity of working caregivers is more than $33 billion per year. The average caregiver costs an employer $2,110 per year. The findings in the 2006 study represent an increase of about $4 billion in both categories from 1997, when the study was first conducted.

12. For practices on measuring performance in virtual work environments, see Igbaria, Devine, and Cheon. "The Measurement of Telecommuting Performance." *Managing Web Usage in the Workplace: A Social, Ethical and Legal Perspective.* Idea Group Publishing, 2002.

13. Zelinsky, M. *New Workplaces for New Workstyles.* McGraw Hill, 1997. Still one of the best discussions of the implications of virtualization on workplace design, workplace sociology, and worker productivity.

14. Simmons, S. *Flexible Working: A Strategic Guide to Successful Implementation and Operation.* Kogan Page, 1996. According to Avery and Zabel, Simmons sorts topics into areas of competency that include "task competencies" (p. 115).

15. Chan, S. "The Invisible Factors in Telecommuting." *Workforce Management,* March 1, 2006. www.workforce.com/ archive/ feature/22/22/78/index_printer.php (registration required). Chan lays out some best practices for managing telecommuting workers and explains how employment terms and measurement differ from those for workers at the traditional workplace.

16. As an example, the virtual learning site Training-classes.com lists a course called Managing a Virtual Office, with a brief description reading: "More and more companies are finding that flexibility for employees in both work hours and work location help them attract and retain the best talents and actually improve productivity. This course identifies the potential benefits and pitfalls in managing a 'virtual' workforce, gives guidelines for maintaining communication, monitoring productivity, and encouraging peak performance. There are methods for assuring alignment and consistency, and suggestions for preserving important working relationships without the traditional work structure." www.trainingclasses .com/course_hierarchy/courses/995_Managing_a_Virtual_Office.php

17. Office Depot is one of many office supply and design retailers to offer extensive resources for home-based workers on its Web site at www.officedepot.com/business center.

18. Gartner has observed in a March 2005 report that "60% of organizations that outsource parts of the customer-facing process will encounter customer defections

and hidden costs that outweigh any potential savings they derive from outsourcing" and that "through 2007, 80% of organizations that outsource customer service and support contact centers with the primary goal of reducing cost will fail." www.gartner .com/press_releases/asset_121821_11.html

19. As reported in *The New Scientist,* issue 2497, April 30, 2005. www.newscientist.com/ channel/being-human/ mg18624973.400.

20. "HP Guide to Avoiding Info-Mania," 2005. h40059. www4.hp.com/featurestories/ pdf/HP-Guide-to-Info-Mania.pdf.

21. *InformationWeek,* Jan. 3, 2007. www.informationweek.com/research/showArticle. jhtml?articleID=19680092136.

22. A guide to the provisions of the Sarbanes-Oxley Act can be found online at www.sarbanes-oxley-forum.com.

23. Caldwell, F. "Sarbanes-Oxley Compliance Hits 15 Percent of the 2006 IT Budget." Gartner Inc. Dec. 9, 2005. www.gartner.com/DisplayDocument?ref=g_search&id= 487387

24. Iron Mountain, "Stumbling Blocks on the Way to Privacy Compliance." Nov. 27, 2006. www.itbusinessedge.com/ item/?ci=22240. Referenced in www.privacyjournal.net/ work1.htm

25. KMWorld Staff. "FRCP Compliance—Still a Ways Off." April 26, 2007. www.kmworld.com/Articles/ReadArticle.aspx?CategoryID=61&ArticleID=35982

26. *Ibid.*

27. Tapscott, D. and Ticoll, D. *The Naked Corporation: How the Age of Transparency Will Revolutionize Business.* Free Press, 2003.

28. Or not. According to a report published by SearchVOIP. com, "more than half of corporate instant messaging (IM) users ignore security policies, while roughly 40 percent say it's their right to disregard those policies." Hickey, A. "IM, Skype, P2P Open Security Holes: Survey." SearchVOIP.com, November 14, 2006.

29. Russinovich, M. "Sony, Rootkits, and Digital Rights Management Gone Too Far," on Mark's SysinternalsBlog, Oct. 31, 2005. www.sysinternals.com/blog/2005/10/sony-rootkits-and-digital-rights.html

30. Graham, J. "Firestorm Rages Over Lockdown of Digital Music." *USA Today,* Nov. 13, 2005. www.usatoday .com/tech/news/computersecurity/2005-11-13-digital-rights_x.htm and "Sony to Pull Controversial CDs, Offer Swap." *USA Today,* Nov. 4, 2005.www.usatoday.com/ money/industries/technology/2005-11-14-sony-cds_x.htm

31. U.S. Census Bureau, 2006.

32. "They are the Future—And They're Coming to a Workplace Near You." Lee Rainie, Pew Internet Project, published by Ft.com, September 19, 2006.www.ft.com/cms/s/77851d1247f5-11db-a42e-0000779e2340.html

33. Strauss, W. and Howe, N. *Millennials Rising.* Vintage Books, 2000.

34. Zemke, B., Raines, C., and Filipczak, B., *Generations at Work.* AMACOM, 2000.

35. This also applies somewhat to the earlier "Generation X," as discussed by Ross, *op.cit.*

36. Carol, J. "Integrating Gen-Y into the Workforce." The Boardroom, 2006.

37. Moynagh, M. and Worsley, R. "Reshaping Retirement: Scenarios and Options." *The Futurist,* Sept.–Oct. 2004.

38. *Op. cit.*, Longman, and Schwartz, P. *Inevitable Surprises*. Gotham Books, 2003.

39. A good overview of both perspectives can be found in InfoWorld Special Report, May 5, 2005. www.infoworld.com/reports/SRh1bvisas.html

40. Drucker, P. *Managing in the Next Society*. St Martins Press, 2002.

41. This issue is explored from two sides in "Proprietary Education—Threat or Not?" NEA Research Center Update, September 2004, and "Discovering the Best Education Stocks." *Shareowner*, July/August 2004.

42. Florida, R. *The Rise of the Creative Class*. Basic Books, 2002.

CHAPTER 7

Managing Knowledge and Talent in the New World of Business

S o far we have explored how the driving forces of globalization, networks, demographics, and transparency are creating a new landscape for business and a new world of work for people. This chapter explores how these dynamic themes might influence one of the most important priorities facing organizations in the years ahead: how to effectively manage knowledge across a blended workforce to gain competitive advantage in a dynamic, integrated global marketplace.

This chapter focuses on the broad themes we explored earlier in the book through the lens of *knowledge* and *talent*. We then examine the implications of how those themes may influence the way organizations manage their talent and knowledge to forge closer relationships with customers and partners, turn great ideas into new products and services, and optimize internal processes.

MANAGING KNOWLEDGE IN ONE WORLD OF BUSINESS

Although globalization is moving forward, its pace and ultimate progress are unpredictable. That uncertainty creates a high degree of risk for organizational knowledge.

In an open and global economy (such as the "Freelance Planet" scenario), talented individuals may be attracted to certain geographical locations—a theory propounded by Richard Florida's writings on the "creative class" and its preference for dynamic urban environments with dense cultural infrastructure.[1] However, the ubiquity of global networks ensures that the knowledge possessed by these individuals, regardless of their physical location, remains available, and will likely go not to the highest (economic) bidder, but to the bidder whose culture, practices, and technology provides the best overall environment and experience for the individual. Are companies prepared to compete for talent on the basis of cultural and workstyle choices, career visibility, and challenging work opportunities?

In a more fragmented world like "Continental Drift," knowledge may be locked behind ideological or geopolitical boundaries that are reinforced by information and communications filtering, or in extreme instances, cut off completely. Those parts of the world that reflect a high friction for knowledge transfer present a different set of issues than those in an open, friction-free knowledge economy. How far might closed societies go to open themselves to disruptive new ideas in the name of economic development spurred by innovation in their knowledge economy?

Regardless of the uncertainties associated with freedom or fragmentation, technology-mediated collaborative environments will serve as the hub for learning and knowledge transfer. Company culture will be distributed according to how organizations choose to orchestrate their collaborative environments, not where or how they build their buildings. Even in places where the economic and cultural effects of globalization have not reached local populations, there will always be a local affluent, expatriate, or temporary management segment of the population who use technology to connect to colleagues around the world.

KNOWLEDGE ANYWHERE, ANYTIME

The build-out of wired and wireless broadband on a global scale is a boon to those struggling with knowledge retention and transfer. Rather than concentrating knowledge and talent in single physical locations, ubiquitous broadband increasingly allows people to find information that can help them start learning from anywhere at any time. More importantly, they can connect with other people in real-time when all parties are available, and asynchronously when challenged by time and distance, so that they may learn "just-in-time" and in the context of a current challenge. Although they may need to wait for a reply, they will not need to delay action, defer questions, or suspend dialog. As resources converge, people can quickly apply advice and learning to achieve local results.

Central to the *always on, always connected* theme is the idea of choice about where and when one works. A Microsoft Information Worker Board of the Future[2] member said they view the workplace as something that could be "reduced to the technology that one uses." As the networks and access devices continue to mature and extend their reach across the world, that view will likely become the majority among younger and older workers alike. This attitude toward work reinforces the idea of lifelong learning as boundaries between work and life blur.

KNOWLEDGE IN THE TRANSPARENT ORGANIZATION

Governments, markets, and organized consumer groups are putting regulatory, legal, and social pressure on organizations to expose an unprecedented level of detailed information about their internal practices to satisfy public desire for accountability, while demanding higher levels of privacy for personal data. To comply with these new demands, organizations need to know how and where to find the right information. This is not always easy, especially when information and practices are segmented across multiple repositories.

Regulatory pressures are often the result of knowledge failures. When knowledge transfer is not fluid and efficient, individuals, or entire organizations can take actions that fail to meet regulatory guidelines. From the opportunity perspective, the lack of solid capabilities to transfer knowledge can result in pressure for new regulations, where they might otherwise be avoided by proactively understanding what consumers, customers, or constituencies expect. Knowledge about customer expectations can result in actions by an organization that reveal important process, product, or service information that can help positively engage customers by delivering the information they need to build loyalty and trust.

A lack of transparency may not only pose compliance challenges, but may also impair an organization's ability to gain insights from past performance to guide future strategies. Many technologies can help organizations become more transparent, from policy-based enterprise content management to transparent workflows and distributed business intelligence. Once organizations have greater insight into their own knowledge assets, they can more readily make themselves transparent to customers, government agencies, or other interested parties through a variety of channels. Various subscription services and the ability to expose corporate data more directly to partners and consumers through portals can improve transparency while driving down the cost of compliance.

Technology can certainly help organizations reduce the costs associated with regulatory compliance, but it may also create higher returns as a means for engaging customers, consumers and constituents. It can be used as a way of sharing knowledge that will reinforce the value proposition of the product or service organization seeking to build a relationship with customers and partners.

MANAGING KNOWLEDGE FOR A CHANGING WORKFORCE

When Baby Boomers retire, they will take with them something valuable and difficult to replace: their knowledge, experience, and a set of values and expectations that has shaped the workplace for the past 25–30 years. Not only are there fewer numbers of workers to replace them, but those workers have vastly different attitudes and expectations. The new talent pool joining the workforce is highly skilled and extremely capable of creating value in collaborative work environments and distributed work situations. However, they do not generally share the previous generation's sense of commitment to a particular employer, or the assumption that work comes before other life priorities. For the majority of this emerging group, their work and their jobs are just a part of an integrated view of life.

The Millennial generation enters the workforce with an unsentimental view of the relationship between employers and employees, resulting in attitudes that focus on self-fulfillment, self-realization, and self-accomplishment. Because they have internalized the predictions made about their career arcs—that they might have dozens of different jobs in many different roles and industries over their working lives—younger workers tend to see any given job as a stepping stone to the next opportunity: just one more line in their growing skills portfolio. That means they are less likely to be motivated by climbing the corporate ladder or even viewing a job as more than a paycheck, especially in jobs that require them to invest time mastering arbitrary processes that are not broadly transferrable to their next roles. The Millennials will create a rapid turnover of knowledge that will require new techniques, and great diligence, in order to retain and leverage the knowledge they bring to the workplace, and the knowledge they obtain and create while they are employed.

The way out of the potential spiral of knowledge decay may be found in other strong attributes associated with the Millennials, namely their high affinity for social networking, team collaboration and their expectation of quick rewards, and their propensity to use technology as a tool across all frontiers of their lives. If those elements are combined, distributed teams, working where and when they choose, governed by a clear set of objectives, and using software to amplify their communication capabilities, can help create a dynamic environment where knowledge sharing is rewarded immediately and metrics are visible to management. Technologies such as shared workspaces, workflows, online forms, expertise location, and knowledge networks, and unified communication (e-mail, instant messaging, mobile, and voice telephony, etc.) are as familiar to this generation of "digital natives" as television was to their parents. Likewise, there is the expectation that these technologies will provide some sort of feedback and monitoring to the organizations that deploy them.

This technique of mining knowledge from collaborative environments will be best applied to the kind of unstructured project work that is becoming more common in corporate and government settings, and will be less useful for transaction-driven encounters. In the knowledge economy, however, value will be derived from innovation and rapid response, while cost savings will be derived from the automation of most highly repetitive tasks. In this way, the value of unique knowledge grows, further increasing the need for processes and environments that can take advantage of the knowledge workers have, and capture knowledge during turnover, which will rapidly infuse new employees with knowledge gained from their predecessors.

Organizations that create dynamic environments, empower their employees, and provide state-of-the-art technology may also find lower turnover rates among Millennials. Microsoft's Information Worker Board of the Future, which sought out the opinions of selected "ambassadors" of the emerging generation, identified these characteristics as strong attractors for younger workers.

FROM "KNOWLEDGE MANAGEMENT" TO MANAGING TALENT AND KNOWLEDGE

The first time around, knowledge management wasn't a smashing success. Organizations attempted to leverage the expertise, experience, and insights of their workers by capturing them in large, structured data systems where they could be easily accessed and retrieved. Unfortunately, these systems were often cumbersome and difficult for people to incorporate into their daily routine. Even when they successfully captured knowledge, the end result was not easy to consume. It was never easy to picture a young hire spending hours in a videotape library listening to the wisdom of elders, and it is even less likely going forward, given the nonlinear learning styles of today's young workers. All of this lead to low levels of participation and abandoned knowledge bases. Workers also became suspicious that their own positions might be at risk once they shared their personal insights and knowledge. In some organizations, the traditional structures of compensation were not set up to reward people who took the time to learn, share, and mentor.

Major social and economic developments over the past ten years are fueling renewed interest in knowledge and talent management techniques. The global economy has driven home the critical role of knowledge as a competitive differentiator. Knowledge is now at least a co-equal capital asset, alongside financial and physical capital, in the creation of value. Access and prompt utilization of distinctive knowledge is proving decisive in every organization's efforts to create innovative new products and services, improve operations, forge more rewarding relationships with partners, and provide outstanding customer service.

The movement toward more customized customer experiences, global research, and demands for rapid response has made work itself less predictable and more complex. Even routine, structured task roles now require a significant component of unstructured knowledge work—*ad hoc* collaboration with colleagues, customers, and partners, open-ended information search, exception-handling, and the construction of personalized "microprocesses" to simplify and automate specific repetitive tasks that fall outside the defined steps of the larger workflow. Traditional knowledge management has achieved its most recognized successes to date precisely in structured task environments like call centers. However, anyone who has interacted with a scripted call center worker on a problem that falls outside the scope of the organization's knowledge base recognizes the limitations of failing to provide workers with the skills and resources to manage the unexpected, the exceptional, or the complex.

Change today happens too fast for people and organizations to rely exclusively on structured processes and the rigid IT solutions that support them. Agility requires that organizations equip all their people—even those in task-based roles—with tools to operate effectively in a knowledge environment: that is, with tools to create, find and share knowledge easily and naturally, within the context of their familiar, daily activities.

Organizations today now have the means, motive, and opportunity to transform the way they manage knowledge and thereby improve their ability to compete effectively in a globally-integrated, networked world. With improved connections between people, more organic models for information storage and retrieval and the democratization of business intelligence, organizations can more effectively manage some of their most pressing problems around innovation, productivity, customer retention, supply management, and regulatory compliance. And as today's cutting-edge technologies begin to surface in mainstream information work applications over the next ten years, the potential returns on knowledge capital will only continue to increase.

COMPLEXITY AND SPECIALIZATION

The term "information worker" increasingly calls for more precision and nuance as technologies, processes, and sciences become more specific. Complexity comes from two sources: the evolution of a system or process over time; and from an increasing amount of information about the underlying structures of processes, markets, and relationships. Some things that appear simple may actually be complex, but until we view them at a higher resolution, we are not exposed to that complexity. Information technology gives us a powerful lens for exploring the complexities of systems whose behavior seems almost random in the abstract. Computers have provided us with insights about physical sciences, statistics, economics, and medicine that would have been undiscoverable without the power to account for billions of variables and unfathomable amounts of raw data. Complexity and specialization force individuals to access and retain highly contextual knowledge in order to succeed.

The tension between complexity and simplification has tangible impacts on work and management. Sometimes it is desirable to view issues in their full complexity, as a way of coming to grips with the level of effort necessary to address them, or for testing tactical proposals to minimize the possibility of unintended consequences. Other times, it is more useful to strip away detail and view situations at a high level of abstraction, where it is possible to see larger trends and causalities. A sales manager, for example, may want detailed status reports on each of his active accounts. The vice president of sales may simply need to see the comparative performance of different sales territories represented as colors on a map. The amount of desirable complexity therefore varies by role and context, so the tools for visualization should be flexible.

Let Experts be Experts

Ideally, organizations would prefer everyone be an expert, or at least proficient, in everything. For obvious reasons, that's not possible. This challenges organizations to allocate the finite expertise and attention of each worker in ways that are optimized for their role and skill.

No one wants untrained generalists doing work that requires specialized skills and experience. This manifests as incompetence—a toxic quality in any workforce, especially one that drives value through knowledge. Equally, but not as obviously harmful, is the problem of specialists forced into the role of generalists. Organizations pay a premium for workers with specialized knowledge, experience, education, and other qualities. When those workers are forced to spend the majority of their productive hours on activities that don't require or develop their special skills—such as when doctors spend more time filling out insurance forms than treating patients, or project managers spend 40 percent of their time searching for information scattered across various repositories—organizations lose the value of their investment (and the person's skills may diminish as a result of disuse or frustration). The productivity and effectiveness of the knowledge-based enterprise falls short of potential, and possibly short of competitive muster.

In the knowledge economy, specialists will demand higher salaries than generalists, and demographic pressures will make specialists increasingly scarce. That dynamic makes the effective utilization of specialists within an organization even more imperative. At the same time, the rewards of specialization create incentives among workers to acquire skills that empower value, as happened with Web expertise in the early days of the dot-com boom.

SIMPLIFYING THE KNOWLEDGE WORK ENVIRONMENT

Organizations can improve the management of their human capital by enabling knowledge transfer and the productive application of expertise through simplification of the information work environment. Simplification can be achieved at different levels, ranging from personal information management to team knowledge sharing to simplification of business processes and workflows.

Personal Knowledge Management

Automation of rote information work processes such as status reporting, project notifications, e-mail filtering, information, and attention management can reduce the burden of "information overload" (e.g., excessive complexity in the information space) and free up the valuable attention of skilled professionals to add maximum value. People will have more time to share knowledge and collaborate with their colleagues, customers and partners.

Organizations that reduce the friction of learning by automating mundane tasks and enabling information exchange will give experts more time to develop their expertise and more time to share it with others. These organizations will not only remove barriers to productivity for their best performers, but also grow their base of knowledge capital by encouraging up-skilling of workers at all levels.

Managing Team Knowledge in a Collaborative Environment

Small teams, whether they are collocated or geographically distributed, face challenges as to how they share process knowledge and individual expertise. Integrated collaboration platforms help team members coordinate their activities using shared workspaces, calendar and schedule services. Presence data for real-time communications helps bridge the challenges of time and distance, while subscription services and automated alerts help ensure awareness of new information or the need for immediate action. Teams can also build process knowledge into the workspace environment with facilities to assign workflow tasks (e.g., document review and research) in the context of their collaborative work.

Embedding Knowledge in Structured Processes

As noted earlier, workers in structured environments such as call centers benefit from flexible knowledge management systems that augment their existing IT applications. These can include tools for ad hoc communication, open-ended information search, and informal environments for capturing and sharing tacit knowledge, such as blogs and wikis.

Simplification Increases Knowledge Utility

It is important that organizations build a means for attracting talent that can meet their needs for specialized services, and those who can fathom the complexity of the systems or services that they develop, deploy, or service. And they need to create environments and work experiences where people can embrace new learning to upgrade their skills, and to obtain knowledge as it is created—all of which will be taking place in a globally distributed workforce. Integrated collaboration and communication can simplify the way people interact, helping them adapt more rapidly to change, either by avoiding risk, or identifying areas of insight that will lead to new opportunities.

TOWARD A DYNAMIC KNOWLEDGE ENVIRONMENT

To manage knowledge and talent in a dynamic business, you need a Dynamic Knowledge Environment (DKE): that is, one with a core set of capabilities that can easily adapt to new business requirements and scenarios quickly and easily, while reusing existing IT investments and end-user skills. If you take into account the dramatic developments in communications and collaboration over the past two decades, much of the infrastructure required to deploy a DKE already exists. These environments, however, often offer point solutions to a particular facet of the knowledge management problem—business intelligence or search, for example—without considering the organic ways in which organizations create, transfer, and retain knowledge. Failure to recognize the organic nature of learning leads to higher information technology costs, the addition of superfluous processes, and a situation that may make it harder for organizations to obtain a unified view of their knowledge assets with each new investment they make.

In many cases, organizations looking for practical solutions for individual needs will fail to create a generalized technology environment that can be used to solve the majority of knowledge capture and retention issues. Enterprise content management (ECM) is one example of this. Because the demand to manage and control the output of a process is so great in some regulatory environments, organizations implementing solutions like ECM often lose their more subtle knowledge such as: knowledge about the process, knowledge about the intermediary forms of content, knowledge about how decisions were made, and what information was used to inform a decision. The complexity of the tactical objective—compliance—overrides general knowledge-sharing as a priority.

IT Priority: Reduce Complexity

From an IT management standpoint, the increasing number of components in a software infrastructure may overwhelm those implementing such systems, forcing them to look for low-hanging fruit, and being satisfied with small wins rather than tackling the larger issues of knowledge transfer and retention. This perfectly rational way of looking at IT issues, however, does not serve the business well in the long-term. A truly comprehensive knowledge management solution requires a systemic overview of both technology and organizational practices to find out where knowledge is being created, how it is being transferred, where it is being stored, and by whom.

The picture that emerges can be frustrating. The difficulty is that knowledge management has no focal point; no single center of gravity around which it revolves. People, processes, information, and culture, in all of their aspects, can act at one time as creator of knowledge, and at another as consumer. At different points in processes, exceptions may require knowledge that could not be anticipated by process designers. And people routinely learn things, discover new information, or realize an insight outside of the structure of a process, a role, or even an organization—and that knowledge must somehow find its way to the right people at the right time, or inversely, be found by the right people at the time they need it.

Attributes of the DKE

In traditional logic diagrams, functions and their interfaces are clear and precise. Handoffs are well defined and interactions invoked when necessary. In the dynamic knowledge environment, though the technical need remains for well defined interfaces and open standards for information flow, the conceptual view of such an environment must necessarily reflect the blurred edges and confused boundaries that exist in real life.

We have seen this type of blurring on the desktop as applications invoke one another to embed spreadsheets into word processing documents or charts into presentations. In the knowledge environment, repositories become more universal. Rather than segregating work by function or role, the dynamic knowledge environment indexes across the boundaries of team-specific or function-specific repositories to create unified views of information. And because the architecture of the dynamic knowledge environment is horizontal by design, knowledge-specific repositories, such as lessons learned, best practices, and communities of practice, use the same mechanisms for implementation as line-of-business tools, further decreasing the dimensions of the data footprint that must be traversed to find the right information.

At the core of the DKE are four primary functional blocks with permeable edges. The first is the *device-centric view*, where the knowledge workers execute their communication and collaboration activities, and where they author or assemble content. This is traditionally seen as a set of applications running on a desktop or notebook computer, but in the future, such an environment may well be a set of services that complement client software to achieve a goal.

Below that is the *information and collaboration integration platform*, which supports workflow, data integration, blogs, wikis, shared calendars, and shared tasks.

The final two pieces of internal infrastructure are comprised of *communications and repository services*, both of which should be transparent and completely integrated with the client experience. In other words, if a knowledge worker saves content, the experience of where that content is saved on the service should be transparent through normal file services. And if communication is required, access to communication facilities should be available wherever needed, and should be able to be invoked from any place a person's name appears.

NAVIGATING THE DYNAMIC KNOWLEDGE ENVIRONMENT

The fluid movement of knowledge through the DKE can best be illustrated through several classic knowledge management capabilities.

Lessons Learned/Best Practices

The core of knowledge management is gaining access to the unique and specific knowledge that people have obtained in the course of doing business. This requires the affirmative participation of people to contribute to the knowledge base—a potential stumbling block to implementation in organizations that lack the culture or the practical incentives for workers to share their knowledge. *KMWorld* magazine cites the example of the legal profession as one that stands to benefit enormously from a DKE, but has been hampered by the financial model that emphasizes billable hours as the primary success metric.[3] So long as members of the firm are not compensated (or, worse, are penalized) for time they take to contribute knowledge to the internal repository, they are unlikely to bother. In this case, any implementation of DKE technology must be accompanied by some kind of shift in the financial model or culture.

However, the right technology approach can also lower barriers to participation. A robust DKE accommodates many ways for people to contribute, depending on their workstyle, and many ways for organizations to promote participation. Increasingly, professional services organizations such as law firms, are creating specific roles to support knowledge creation, learning and retention. For example, many leading UK firms have well-developed precedents and know-how systems. These are maintained by full-time professional support lawyers (PSLs) who are senior lawyers (and in some cases partners), and who are experts in their fields. The functions of PSLs, depending on the firm and the practice group, may include: development of precedents, maintenance of know-how databases, filtering and dissemination of current awareness information, and training.[4]

Organizations can promote blogs, wikis, and internal discussion forums where valuable contributors receive recognition and reward. The information shared in these forums is self-organizing (for example, a blog about software installation issues, or a discussion group on contract case law), and also searchable within the knowledge repository.

A DKE should also simplify the process of user contributions by allowing input via unstructured data (voice, video, handwritten notes), from devices ranging from desktop PCs to phones, faxes, scanned documents or notes taken on a TabletPC, and enable that information to be searchable using metadata tags or pattern recognition.

People elsewhere in the organization could then subscribe to subjects of interest via subscriptions, using tools like RSS feeds. Such feeds would allow them to expose frequently-used resources on personalized portal sites, receive notifications via e-mail, voicemail, or other preferred channels, or access knowledge using research and discovery functions built in to their information work productivity software.

And in the DKE, lessons learned and best practices are not static. As soon as they are shared, individuals within the organization can modify them, apply them in different ways, and share their learning and the context of their applications to further enhance the knowledge infrastructure of their organization or community.

Improved Access to Information

Improved search and file management technologies in the DKE remove the artificial layer of abstraction in the "folder and directory" model and allow people to find information according to meaningful content tags, whether it's stored locally or in a network repository. In the example above, the analyst would simply type in "Q2 financials spreadsheet" and get pointers to all relevant files, wherever they reside.

This also addresses the problem of static data taxonomies, where the structure of the database can't keep pace with changing requirements and soon overwhelms the ability of users and IT to maintain the growing list of classifications. Organizations can achieve this benefit—not through the physical consolidation of all data assets into a single place—but through services that expose data from multiple locations as a single logical repository for search. In a DKE, the search function is available across all applications and devices, and can be embedded and invoked from within applications so people don't have to leave their work context to find information.

Finding the Right People

When people, rather than data or documents, are the objects of search, the same challenges and solutions apply. Organizational roles and titles serve the same problematic function as file folders within a rigid taxonomy—they tell only part of the story. Meaningful knowledge and expertise can exist throughout an organization without regard for formal divisions of labor. Knowledge networks can help expose hidden assets by connecting people to the processes, discussions, documents, and projects that can help them achieve a goal or complete a task with more proficiency. At the same time, knowledge networks allow them to reveal their ability to contribute by passively identifying expertise and competence from the work they contribute and the conversations in which they take part.

A DKE provides several ways to locate and engage the right people. Expertise identifiers can be built into the organizational contacts directory, and those contacts can be automatically included in discussions or notifications via RSS and other publish-subscribe models. Project managers can rapidly find and build teams based on expertise, reputation, past performance, and history of interaction with other team members. For *ad hoc* communication, presence information is embedded in documents, processes, team sites, and e-mail, indicating whether the person is available for real-time communication (whether instant message, phone/videoconference, or a meeting), all of which can be called upon, or switched between, from the same, familiar interface.

Distributed Mentoring and Coaching

Person-to-person knowledge transfer is often the most efficient and effective. But as with mediated knowledge, there is the problem of incentives and culture. If the process of mentoring and coaching is too burdensome for the participants—particularly the mentor/coach—the opportunity for learning may be lost.

A DKE provides easy, natural ways for people to impart knowledge in one-to-one or one-to-many situations. Real-time communication via instant message, online meetings, and remote application-sharing sessions provides direct opportunities for dialog, demonstration, and feedback. People can also use presence status to indicate their availability—or lack thereof—to set up a kind of "office hours" for consultation and set aside other time for uninterrupted work or personal time. Presence also supports "just-in-time learning" by connecting parties at the exact time the knowledge is needed.

A DKE can facilitate specialized e-learning opportunities through its rich collaboration and communication capabilities. This type of e-learning would leverage the existing capabilities of the infrastructure, rather than requiring organizations to duplicate their investments with closed, proprietary systems.

Blog comment threads, wikis, and discussion forums provide channels for asynchronous knowledge transfer. Many organizations have implemented these kinds of channels to provide IT helpdesk services, sometimes in combination with real-time chat and application sharing. The same practices could easily apply to other types of specialized knowledge.

Driving Innovation

Innovation in practice means the design and refinement of products, services, and processes. As this is fundamentally a knowledge-based activity, a DKE offers many ways to speed and simplify the process while improving the quality of the output.

Routing, notification, version control, and all the other routine tasks that are part of the product development cycle can be automated, saving participants the time and trouble of managing administrative activities. The tools to design and modify processes, such as forms and workflow diagrams, are part of the information/work application environment, so the team members and management can adapt process rules to fit changing conditions and work styles without involving IT.

The primary advantage of a DKE is the ability to embed knowledge into processes. At each point in the process, participants have access to the people and information they need to maximize their contribution. All the knowledge within the organization can be brought to bear on problem-solving, leading to innovative solutions that incorporate the best, most up-to-date expert and customer feedback.

Learning from Customers

Many organizations gather customer data from transactions. Data, however, is not the same as knowledge. Raw data must be assembled from the various repositories in which it is collected (CRM systems, transaction systems, loyalty programs, sales and marketing lists, sales force automation applications, etc.), then interpreted to determine a course of action. Because of the sheer volume of data that organizations now collect, there is the real risk that the prescriptive or predictive quality of the information could be obscured in a welter of complexity.

A DKE assists people in using customer data by allowing them to customize the way they consume it according to their needs and role. When data is accessible and pervasive across the entire enterprise, organizations can build dashboards and alerts into personalized workspaces, and provide customer-facing workers with a single view of the relationship to provide better service. In most cases, the individual workers will be able to assemble the information they need from high-level components that fit easily into their existing information management tools, be it their e-mail client or their personal portal.

Organizations can also obtain knowledge from customers who require less abstraction and interpretation. They can ask them directly for their views and engage them in a dialog. This can provide invaluable insights to all kinds of processes from product design to service delivery, while also forging a closer relationship with customers. However, customers can face some of the same barriers to contributing information as internal employees: lack of incentive and lack of opportunity. A DKE provides organizations with ways to reach out to customers as part of an interactive process, through blogs, private community sites, social networks, Webcasts, questionnaires, and events: a wide range of informal, interactive conversations that can engage and reward customers, while providing genuine and contextual learning opportunities for product teams and service providers.

People as Process

The so-called 80/20 rule in business states that 20 percent of transactions are exceptions to normal processes, but consume 80 percent of the resources. Obviously, it is advantageous to gradually evolve processes to capture more and more exceptions. At the same time, it is virtually impossible to design a process that anticipates every potential outcome, especially with the kind of complex, knowledge-intensive needs that many organizations now face, both internally and externally. There will always be a need for people to apply their knowledge, training, and discretion to resolve issues, and in any process, there is likely to be a need to escalate or engage outside expertise from time to time.

A DKE embraces people as part of structured processes and enables them to access the resources they need—information, expertise, escalation, or secondary processes—in a more flexible and responsive way. Search and collaboration services are available to workers from within structured workflow applications, so exception-handling tasks can be accomplished without leaving the familiar integrated work environment. When people are empowered as a part of process-driven work, organizations can achieve the predictability and economy of structure, combined with the responsiveness and adaptability that only people can provide.

Making Better Decisions

Business Intelligence (BI) offers executives a view into enterprise data to support decision making—a critical capability in a dynamic, competitive marketplace. And there is considerable overlap between the capabilities of BI systems and the knowledge transparency features of a DKE. The risk is that organizations that invest in dedicated BI solutions without consideration of the whole knowledge creation, transfer, and retention ecosystem—not to mention use of collaborative tools to rapidly disseminate and assimilate insights garnered from a BI system—may end up with significantly greater IT cost and complexity, duplicated capabilities, and fundamental system incompatibilities. Additionally, they may also experience lost opportunities from insights that just couldn't find their way to someone who could act on them.

Building a holistic DKE that includes collaboration, content management, forms, portal integration, unified communication and search, in addition to core BI capabilities, enables organizations to mobilize a greater volume of knowledge for decision-support than traditional BI systems. And this occurs in an open, interoperable environment where decision-support information can be incorporated into standard or customized applications for easy use and access.

Facilitating Communities of Practice

Communities of Practice are a way for geographically distributed organizations or informal groups to share, transfer, and retain information using DKE facilities such as team workspaces, threaded discussion groups, online meetings, document repositories, interactive live meetings, and other collaborative forums. In addition to encouraging mutual learning and sharing of best practices, communities can be a hedge against workforce transition. The community repository retains not only the knowledge exchanged by the members, but the entire context of discussion and feedback. New team members can familiarize themselves with the whole institutional background of particular subjects by combing through community archives, and therefore reduce the time it takes to ramp up to full participation. In active communities, the role of mentoring is often distributed among the group, rather than managed through top-down HR processes, transforming the community into the *de facto* repository for knowledge in terms of both human capital and intellectual property.

Measuring Knowledge Utilization

By centralizing the knowledge infrastructure, organizations not only gain the benefits of efficient information search and transfer, but also the ability to observe and measure patterns of search, communication, collaboration, contribution, and process performance. Managers can apply visualization tools to collaboration metadata, which will help them identify the *real* distribution of work and expertise within their organization. This can help bring formal policies in line with effective practices. They can also employ download statistics, blog traffic measurements, and reputation systems (to grade the usefulness of individual contributions) to assign relative value to their knowledge assets, whether they are documents, systems or people.

EMBRACING ORGANIZATIONAL LEARNING

Technology is important as a means of connecting people in the *new world of business*, for capturing the output of their creativity and for providing them the information crucial to the decisions they make. Still, it is not the only necessary component for a strong learning environment.

The success of learning and talent retention in the future will depend on an organizational commitment to a *culture of learning.* Knowledge contributors should be recognized and rewarded. Incentive structures should be examined and modified to encourage people to develop their own skills and those of their colleagues through collaboration, discussion, mentoring, and communities of practice.

As demographics trends, globalization, and technology advances accelerate the workforce transition, organizations must act quickly to preserve their knowledge. A DKE points toward one way technology could create a comprehensive capability to create, transfer, and retain knowledge, based on a rational and cost-effective IT infrastructure.

Organizations should look beyond the tactical solution categories of business intelligence, portals, search, workflow, and others, and think about the business productivity infrastructure as a whole. In that way, organizations can begin moving toward the benefits of a Dynamic Knowledge Environment in a systematic, economical way.

10 STARTING POINTS FOR DYNAMIC KNOWLEDGE ENTERPRISES

1. Encourage *informal knowledge capture* through the use of collaborative technology that works the way people work.
2. Deploy *flexible and adaptable technology* that amplifies the capabilities of employees by helping them quickly find the people, processes, or information they need to be effective.
3. Allow employees to invest in relationships and use their *social networks* for learning and knowledge sharing.
4. *Align incentive and reward programs* to encourage knowledge sharing.
5. *Embrace innovation* throughout the organization as a focal point for organizational learning and action
6. *Build knowledge networks* with employees, partners, and customers that help anticipate future demand and risks.

7. Build an information architecture that allows the organization to *optimize around people, not process*, so that people can collaborate, find and use information, and build work-saving tools within the natural context of their role, task, and workstyle.

8. Consider the role space plays in knowledge exchange and *create physical environments that encourage knowledge sharing*.

9. Include the recognition of knowledge intensive processes and the retention of talent and knowledge as a *specific goal in strategic planning*.

10. *Define metrics* in the context of strategic organizational goals that will demonstrate the value of knowledge investments.

NOTES

1. Florida, R. *The Rise of the Creative Class.* Basic Books, 2002.
2. Rasmus, D. W. "Information Workers of the Future at Microsoft." *KM Review,* Vol. 7, Issue 5, November/ December 2005.
3. McKeller, H. "Business and Practice: KM and the Law." KM World, September 29, 2006. www.kmworld.com/ Articles/ReadArticle.aspx?ArticleID=18280 www.llrx.com/features/benchmarkingkm.htm
4. www.llrx.com/features/benchmarkingkm.htm

CHAPTER **8**

The Future of Industries

The broad social and economic trends transforming the world of work and business have specific implications in particular industries. For example, transparency and regulation are already driving numerous and obvious changes in the way financial services firms operate. Global supply networks and trade liberalization have transformed commodity manufacturing into a race to the bottom of the wage scale, forcing manufacturing sectors of developed economies to rely on innovation and execution as competitive differentiators. Pervasive networks and distributed information systems are speeding the adoption of long-hoped-for innovations in healthcare such as electronic medical records and evidence-based medicine. Numbers show that the aging workforce will hit the public sector especially hard, with some government agencies due to lose more than 70 percent of their current workforce to retirement by 2012.

As part of our work, we applied our scenario-planning model to different industries based on their unique dynamics and requirements.

We also looked at the gamut of technology innovations in communications, networks, software, and infrastructure, and thought about how they would manifest as part of the information work environment over the next 10–15 years. Specifically, how will technology such as semantic search, smart content, full-spectrum collaboration and communication, visualization and simulation, location services, and physical object data be incorporated into the work experience of ordinary people in industry-specific roles, such as plant manager, healthcare provider, branch bank teller, or government worker? And how will the broader access to people, process, and information ripple through the management structure, flattening hierarchical organizations, blurring the boundaries of the workplace and workday, changing modes of communication, and influencing decision-making?

This chapter summarizes the results of our forecasting process, plotting the intersection of global dynamics, technological innovation, and the possibility of disruptive events across six industry segments: manufacturing, retail, government/public sector, banking and insurance, healthcare, education, and professional services. These investigations were originally presented in a series of white papers from 2006 to 2008, which explored the issues in greater depth, and are available at www.microsoft.com.

MANUFACTURING

In high-wage, high-value-add economies, the survival of manufacturing depends on leveraging the skills and talents of the workforce, not to merely drive down costs of production (an uphill battle in competition with commodity producers in emerging economies), but to create new value through innovation. Key themes in the future of manufacturing include:

Innovating for leadership: Manufacturers live and die by their capability to bring new products to the market quickly. To succeed in this competitive environment, a company's people must collaborate with suppliers, engineers, and product designers using shared platforms to exchange ideas. However, traditional top-down innovation models that rely on a small group of experts to generate ideas are no longer enough. Manufacturers will need to open the innovation process to a much wider community, including production workers, partners, outside experts, and customers. Social computing technologies that enable user-created content, communities of practice, and distributed project management can help management spot the most promising potential innovations and streamline them into production.

Optimizing operations: Manufacturers at all points in the value chain, from leading innovators to low-cost providers, must constantly optimize their performance to remain competitive with others in their niche in a global market. Companies that build their success on operational excellence provide ready and easy-to-use technologies to empower their people to be highly efficient. In the data-driven manufacturing operation, traditional enterprise resource planning (ERP) systems provide a real-time view of everything from sales orders to plant-floor operations. Increasingly, that information can be integrated with external sources of data from GPRS systems, financial markets, marketing lists, and so on, and then presented in customized views (such as mashups or dashboards) that give managers visibility to make decisions faster and improve productivity.

Forging stronger value chain partnerships: One thing that the experience of the past several years has shown us is that global brands are only as strong as their suppliers. When a downstream supplier fails to meet quality requirements, as occurred recently in cases involving toys, pet food, and other consumer products, it is the global brand that pays the price in lost trust and regulatory exposure. An important part of working in a dynamic business environment and a global marketplace involves working closely with suppliers and industry partners to reduce time-to-market, to manage inventory and replenish parts as needed, and to share financial responsibility and risks if markets shift. With the right hardware and software, people can manage complex relationships with multiple partners to produce quality, error-free products, and higher profitability.

Driving higher-value customer relationships: Any manufacturer can benefit from a deeper connection with its customers. But to achieve these connections, the manufacturer's employees must have the tools to meet their commitment to serve customers well. Customer relationships management (CRM) systems provide the foundation for these capabilities by delivering a unified view of the customer relationship for sales and service employees. Increasingly, manufacturers will extend beyond traditional CRM to build richer, more collaborative relationships over the Web, using structured (e-business sites, forms, order tracking) and unstructured (blogs, service wikis, support forums) services to provide information and connectivity.

RETAIL

As the retail business has become more global and sophisticated, the core activities of retail—merchandising, store/site operations, supply management, finance, marketing and human resources—have become increasingly information-based to drive standardization and efficiency. Buyers can now search the world for the right products and prices. Retailers in a more competitive global market also need increasingly distinctive brand identities to attract and retain market share. This means creating a unique customer experience through merchandise mix, customer service, advertising, pricing, and the store environment (either physical or online), and reinforcing it through consistent execution across geographies and media. Many retailers are looking at innovative in-store technology to provide greater customer convenience and increase the capabilities of sales associates to offer personalized service.

Reinventing the Retail Experience

To respond to consumer needs as well as market and industry changes, retailers must be agile to take advantage of technologies that enable a seamless workflow driven by demand. This implies a technology infrastructure that is based on true data management. In the future, technology will enable a single view of the customer across all channels, and retailers will need to stop looking at the data and instead focus on the architecture that houses it. The supply chain as we know it will be more consumer-focused, and collaboration will support the customer experience rather than just cost reduction. Both will be accomplished through the integration of disparate systems embedded throughout business operations. When radio-frequency identification (RFID) technology comes of age in the next decade, retailer-supplier collaboration will become a catalyst for operational innovation that enables seamless workflow at the business process and human levels.

Cocreating the Global Marketplace

In the consumer-driven economy, customers expect to transact business without boundaries. They want the kind of convenience enabled by location-based awareness, enhanced mobility, and RFID capabilities: expectations that accelerate every time an early-adopter successfully implements one of these technologies online or in-store. For retailers and the consumer product industry, this means real-time integration around the supply chain. Innovation in retail will move out of the executive corridor and into the front lines of the business, where manufacturers, distributors, retailers, and consumers interact. In the area of advertising, more companies are bypassing traditional channels and marketing directly to their customers through cell phones, text messaging, instant messaging (IM), online click-throughs, and one-to-one personalization. The supply chain as we know it will be more consumer-focused, and collaboration will support the customer experience rather than cost reduction.

Evolving Toward Next-Generation Sales and Service

Integration and collaboration are critical to people in every role of the enterprise. These affect retailers on two fronts: employees and suppliers. The future will be about getting more technology into the hands of employees to improve productivity, provide supply-chain visibility, and create a better work experience. For suppliers, it will be about real-time access to demand data. Both, ultimately, will improve the customer experience, build loyalty, and generate repeat business.

GOVERNMENT/PUBLIC SECTOR

Government processes are static by design, opaque by legislative require-ment, detached from the dynamics of the free market by definition, and based on lagging technology infrastructure due to resource limitations. The problem is that public-facing government agencies serve the same customers and draw from the same workforce as the rest of society, and people inevitably bring some of their expectations from their experience as consumers and information workers to their dealings with govern-ment. To succeed in the 21st century, governments need to be responsive to change, transparent and accountable, and convenient for citizens and businesses, even within the constraints that distinguish the public sector from private enterprise. They need to draw correct inferences from data, act rapidly, and recognize and change course if necessary. The problems of a complex, interconnected world require governments to get the max-imum benefit from their knowledge assets—not just from data records, but also from process knowledge, human expertise, and unstructured content.

Among the priorities for the new world of government work:

Expanding participation: Many governments have already moved basic transactional functionality (license applications, tax filing, and so on) to the Web. The next step is to improve participation and compliance by making access to government information, people, and processes easier for people anywhere in the country, by using richer, more interactive and collaborative channels to engage citizens and businesses.

Doing more at lower cost: Every government faces resource con-straints that apply despite rising demand for government services and higher expectations from the public. Governments can improve their productivity and capabilities by giving citizens, policy-makers, managers, and teams better access to information and better tools for oversight and accountability. This includes using service-based architectures to integrate legacy data sources, simplifying access to data and applications using secure Web-based forms and interfaces, and making process and workflows more visible.

Facilitating transparency while protecting citizen privacy: Governments have a special responsibility to balance the benefits of openness and collaboration with the privacy rights of citizens. Perimeter security (firewalls, disconnected systems) and process safeguards protect data, but also make it extremely difficult to achieve qualitative and performance improvements that require the free exchange of information between trusted partners. Content-level security that uses information rights management and metadata inherent in individual documents and portions of documents simplifies the management requirements for sensitive data while ensuring that only authorized users have access to protected information, and that chain-of-custody and retention policies can be audited and enforced.

Improving policy outcomes: Public policy makers can benefit from the same quantitative, data-driven practices that are revolutionizing business processes elsewhere in the economy, helping to align practices within a department to the policy vision. Government agency executives, armed with key performance indicators linked to real-time data from internal systems and external data sources, can not only make better management decisions with respect to allocating resources, but also pursue or curtail activities according to changing social circumstances (e.g., shift police resources to neighborhoods where the crime rate is edging up, clarify documentation that is generating high numbers of inquiries to agency staff, and so on).

RETAIL BANKING AND INSURANCE

Global dynamics are forcing change on an industry rooted in time-tested practices and traditional business culture. Sophisticated customers are demanding more choices, increased transparency in areas such as services, fees, rates and claims, and greater convenience. Governments and markets are demanding transparency and adherence to strict safeguards related to data, risk and reserving, sales, and other business practices. Competition is emerging from new players with new business models and nontraditional delivery processes. In addition, long-held assumptions about the place of retail banks, full-service brokers, and insurance companies in the value chain are suddenly open to question.

Despite all of these pressures, the big change in the financial services industry has not happened yet. Centuries-old models and cultures persist at many leading firms, and strategic planning efforts remain focused on traditional sources of competition and growth. There is an enormous opportunity for those banks and insurers who can get out ahead of the curve, through agile systems and processes that will allow them to react more quickly and effectively to unexpected change than the competition. Financial services organizations will be challenged to:

- **Create new business models** that transform banking and insurance from a reactive business to one that cocreates value with customers through customized offerings and proactive risk management.

- **Turn static data into dynamic assets** by integrating information stored in legacy systems, acquired through mergers, or shared via partnerships, then providing personal bankers, underwriters, adjusters, and managers with a single view across all the business data.

- **Embrace new delivery models** that reflect customers' desire to do business online, via mobile device, or using embedded data and location devices (e.g., OnStar or LoJak in vehicles, or RFID chips in personal property).

- **Empower the next-generation workforce** by putting them in closer collaboration with the people, processes, and information and accommodating their desire for a more flexible integration of work and life.

HEALTHCARE

Cost pressures, new innovations, demographics, new delivery models, and rising expectations are transforming healthcare services around the world. New technology plays a central role in the way providers, patients, and payers will interact with the healthcare ecosystem in the years to come. However, adoption has been slow in many cases, due in part to the nature of healthcare services and the culture of medicine.

As uptake of information work technology expands across the healthcare landscape, it will help relieve many of today's frustrations and challenges. It will support and extend the capabilities of clinicians and healthcare facility administrators. It will bring information smoothly into existing ways of working and reduce the complexity of burdensome processes. The New World of Healthcare Work is characterized by:

- **Rapid spread of effective practices:** Clinicians and administrators will have pervasive access to the latest knowledge to improve outcomes, as technology, expectations, and the attitudes of next-generation healthcare workers drive broader acceptance of evidence-based medicine and research.

- **Better use of healthcare resources:** With less overhead of process complexity and paperwork, hospitals, clinics, and doctors' offices will operate more efficiently and focus their resources on patient care.

- **Rising standards of care worldwide:** The latest innovations in medical science will spread immediately across the professional community and around the world.

- **More even distribution of healthcare:** With telemedicine enabled by collaboration software, pervasive networks, and powerful mobile devices, providers will extend the reach of their skills to even remote, poorly served areas.

- **Focus on preventative care:** Payers will be able to align reimbursement plans to support preventative care and effective treatments without looming over the shoulders of providers and patients.

- **Accessible data with privacy safeguards:** Although medical information and records will be standardized, portable, and accessible at the point of care, privacy and confidentiality are protected by robust content-level security. Governments will need to support patient privacy efforts with effective legislation and regulation to prevent discriminatory practices by payers, especially as genomic data that gives clues to hereditary conditions, becomes part of the patient medical file.

EDUCATION

Like healthcare professionals, educators have always focused on outcomes rather than outputs. Although managing administrative burdens remain an issue, the most critical issues facing today's educators are how to transform the learning experience by effectively incorporating technology so they can discover new insights about students; how to work cooperatively with other educators; and how to bridge gaps in talent that schools share with other geographically centered institutions. They must balance these learning-experience challenges with the demands created by a global market for education, increasing expectations from industry and community, mounting requirements for transparency, and demographic shifts that are affecting the populations of both educators and students.

Helping Educators Learn

Educators have a limited amount of time that they can devote to self-development. Technology can assist educators by giving them an easier way to connect to, and learn from, colleagues around the world through social networks, deliver learning in manageable portions through virtual learning experiences and conferences, and supplement their instructional time with qualified individuals willing to engage their students in alternative learning experiences.

Modeling Learning

The overriding skill required for the 21st century will be the ability to learn. Instructors can tell this to students, but they can effectively instill an appreciation for lifelong learning only by demonstrating it themselves—by learning from one another and from students as a routine part of their professional development: "reciprocal mentoring." Educators with superior technology skills, for instance, can help their peers better incorporate technology into the curriculum—not behind the scenes, but interactively with students watching. Students will learn that their educators need to continue learning by seeing that education process taking place before them.

Scale and Individualization

Whether an educator has five students or 35, it is important to gain insights into the uniqueness of each student. Over the next several years, as student records, achievements, and assignments become increasingly aggregated in tools such as electronic portfolios, educators will employ learning analytics to supplement and validate their own observations about student performance. Learning analytics will allow educators to combine their own insights with those of previous instructors, parents, and administrators so they can better address the individual needs of students.

Rethinking the Classroom and the School Year

The traditional September-to-June school year observed in the northern hemisphere was first instituted in the 19th century to meet the needs of an agrarian society. As we enter a more knowledge-intensive era, some communities and schools are looking for ways to move to year-round learning, though these efforts sometimes meet with resistance. Open learning environments can give education systems greater flexibility by extending the resources of education beyond the traditional school day, year, and physical location.

Simplify Administrative Tasks

With more demands being placed on education by parents, students, employers, and society, educational institutions and educators can benefit greatly from the more extensive implementations of information and communications to speed and simplify routine tasks and facilitate communication. This will help ease the burdens on overworked educators and give them more time to focus on the craft of teaching.

Enable Transparency

Communication—within schools and between schools, parents, and the community—is one area where technology can deliver benefits. Today, many schools still use a disruptive public address system to make announcements during the school day; send paper copies of schedules, bulletins, and permission forms; and use a variety of convoluted systems to communicate grades to students and parents. A number of current and emerging technologies can remove these points of friction, including these examples: subscription services via RSS, online meetings, collaborative workspaces, sharing of data analysis and information rights management to make sure the information is only shared with the parties who should see it.

PROFESSIONAL SERVICES

Professional Services Organizations represent a diverse range of businesses, including accounting practices, architecture and engineering firms, business consultancies, IT service organizations, and law firms. Despite this diversity of specialization, firms have certain objectives in common. They derive value from the skills of their professional practitioners, they need to manage limited resources to maximize revenue, and their long-term success depends on delivering a superior client experience.

Four dynamics shaping the future of professional services include:

1. **Adapting the Professional Services business model to a dynamic world:** The key to flourishing in a world of opportunistic part-

nerships and a constant reshuffling of the marketplace is to keep knowledge within the firm fluid. Both the IT systems and the management practices around knowledge capture, retention, and transfer should reflect the spontaneous, informal, networked reality of the dynamic business world, using emergent social computing models rather than structured knowledge management platforms and approaches.

2. **Selling knowledge, not time:** Intellectual capital is a larger and more durable source of value than fee-based services. Firms can transition from old fee-for-service models to licensees of proprietary intellectual capital by stimulating the creation, reuse, and effective management of their knowledge assets. Technologies such as reputation systems ("rate this page/rate this comment"), collaborative filtering (to expose the most relevant content), and relationship mapping (to identify innovation hot-spots and top contributors in an organization) can assist management in identifying high-value content.

3. **Making value transparent to clients:** Increased competition and changing expectations are challenging the venerable system of hourly billing, the core of the professional services business model. Whether firms choose to stick with the rate card and time sheet, or move to customized systems of value- or project-based pricing, transparency is essential to meet rising expectations of clients, partners, and governments for visibility into the billing, management, and value creation process.

4. **Managing talent in a changing workforce:** Experienced workers are set to retire and newer workers bring different values to the workplace, and the practices necessary to recruit and retain next-generation talent requires more than a competitive compensation package. Millennial-age professional service workers value the opportunity to gain experience and contribute. Mentoring programs, enabled or mediated by collaboration technology, not only facilitate knowledge transfer but also build bonds of culture that assist in retention, motivation, and succession planning down the road.

CHAPTER 9

Hearing the Future

This book is titled *Listening to the Future* and it explores how scenarios have helped shape the way Microsoft views the intersection of technology, people, process, policy and practice.

As the book closes, we thought it would be useful to expand on the explanation of scenario planning offered in the first chapter. We will offer guidance to organizations to enable them not only *listen* to the future, but also *hear* what it has to say.

Many organizations attempt to ponder the implications of trends. Few do it in a systematic way, using established methods. Anyone can brainstorm about possibilities, drawing out futures that are rich in detail and lush with self-serving assumptions. Uncertainties lend themselves to resolution through either/or choices; organizations and individuals are naturally tempted to make the choices that conform to their preexisting beliefs or interests. As emotionally rewarding as these activities may be, they are not a management discipline and can lead to disastrous outcomes if they create a sense of unwarranted confidence in situations that in fact hold significant risk.

Relatively recent techniques like scenario-planning have created frameworks in which organizations can consider the "alternative futures" that might unfold as a result of inherently uncertain, unknowable dynamics playing out in the future. It is important to recognize these tools for what they are: *windtunnels* that help assure a strategy's robustness—and as forcing devices to surface powerful new innovative directions. Scenarios should not be seen as a method for imposing order on the uncertainties that haunt all plans.

Trend watchers must beware that without a strategic framework, they are more susceptible to two tenets of thinking about the future that we have introduced.

Trends do not forecast disruptive events

and

Disruptive events can derail a trend, eradicate it, or render it meaningless.

Anecdotal evidence suggests that organizations occasionally get lucky, in hindsight, and discover that one or more of their trend-watching methods played a role in their ability to anticipate an event, and thereby to capitalize on an opportunity, or overcome a challenge. Taken as a whole, however, most organizations pay precious little attention to the future, and those that do, often do so half-heartedly, haphazardly, and with a consistency that could constitute "organizational attention deficit disorder."

Then, there are organizations that consider their future using robust methods—even if those methods initially produce views of the future that challenge deeply held ideologies, shake the confidence of management, or pose troubling questions for the organization's direction. These organizations embrace uncertainty as part of the vision process. They recognize the value of exposing unseen risk and planning for the widest range of possible futures, not just the pleasing ones.

STRATEGY AND UNCERTAINTIES

Strategy is essentially a model of the world. It is a set of beliefs and values combined with the anticipated results of acting on those beliefs. Those actions may be tactics for marketing current products or services, or they may be social actions that reinforce the belief in order to position an organization in a certain way. Microsoft's work with scenarios and the company's discipline of constantly exploring the underlying assumptions of their model, has led to the idea of *dynamic uncertainty* in which emergent uncertainties may act as a reorganizing vector for scenarios independent of traditional team-based "batch" or "event" reviews of the scenarios and their underlying logics.

When an emergent uncertainty is discovered, the first question is "Does this change our model or does it fit under an existing category?" Uncertainties that demonstrate no ability to fundamentally alter the outcome of the scenarios, or that do not influence other uncertainties by adding richness to the narrative or logic of the scenarios should be discarded. At an even deeper level, the failure of an uncertainty to effect fundamental change may mean that a previously identified uncertainty acts as a proxy for the newer discovered trait. Introducing the new trait would overly complicate the model and not create additional actionable information. It can then be correctly grouped with the larger uncertainty within the scenario framework and discarded as an independent variable. This kind of narrative hygiene is necessary to prevent scenarios from becoming complicated by too many moving parts and losing their clarifying qualities.

If the new uncertainty fundamentally changes the outcomes of the scenarios by adding unique information that enhances the richness of the scenario logic, then it needs to be retained and its interactions with the models explored. This should happen as part of an iterative process. It is rarely necessary to discard an entire scenario framework to accommodate a new uncertainty. However, it sometimes happens that the new uncertainty will resolve or render moot other aspects of the older model—such as the way the discovery of a cheap renewable energy source would tend to change geopolitical models based on access to oil resources. More often, however, rather than single events triggering the collapse into a scenario singularity, the perturbations over time through the introduction of new critical uncertainties will force a model to evolve.

In modern physics, it is currently being argued that there is no such thing as a vacuum of space: at the scale near and below the Plank Length, space is teeming with particles that seemingly emerge from nowhere and rapidly disappear. This could just as easily describe the process of examining the world for emerging uncertainties. And just as technology has not given us the ability to peek into Plank Length behavior in the cosmos, neither has it given us the ability to create models of behavior for economies or organizations that don't fall apart at first contact with reality.

What technology *has* done is expose our current models to reveal the need for a deeper understanding of relationships and causality than before. In the case of business, the increasing interconnectedness and complexity of the global marketplace create an urgent need for greater clarity more rapidly than in the past. The techniques outlined here reinforce a premise that organizations that apply strategic planning principles, and by executing to their ability, by foresight or by strength of position and market power, can help shape the future.

One thing we know is that the number of variables that must be considered for enterprises engaged in global trade has increased. No longer is it sufficient to build out markets based on local biases. The world is far lumpier than it is flat. In global economies, the uncertainties increase as the number of markets and interactions increase, because it is neither possible nor appropriate to assume a common culture either exists or will emerge anytime soon. Organizations must adapt to local market niches to thrive in those markets.

Second thing we know is that the ability to manage uncertainty cannot be thought of as an exercise for organizations in isolation. The process of listening to the future must be the work of an *adaptive community* that has socialized future thinking and can help identify critical uncertainties across a wide range of social, political, economic, technological, and cultural dimensions. This community must be disciplined to observe and engage questions in whose outcome they have a passionate, shared interest.

Third, scenario models, including their underlying constructs, must become dynamic. It is not enough to simply identify and track only selected metrics, in the hope that these few factors alone will provide insights in perpetuity. Dynamic scenario models must be constantly challenged by the emergence of relevant uncertainties that challenge the underlying framework of the model. A robust system for listening to the future must therefore incorporate the means to change, much as a robust system of constitutional government includes mechanisms—albeit stringent ones—for amending a constitution as conditions require. Like amending a constitution, incorporating emergent uncertainties into an existing framework is not, or at least should not be, the first reaction of planners to unexpected conditions. Both the process of honing scenario logics and the profound implications of changing the framework itself, to some degree, create a barrier to the introduction of dynamic uncertainties unless they are truly, undeniably disruptive in ways that can't be accommodated by the existing assumptions.

At the same time, ignoring an uncertainty because it inconveniently challenges the assumptions of the model, or may perturb it in such a way that the model requires an elemental retelling of its associated stories, is to disregard the underlying value of scenarios to act as stories about the future that facilitate strategic dialog. Fixing scenarios in response to new conditions can be time-consuming, but the cost is minimal compared to the problems of relying on the outputs of a framework that is past its sell-by date. It is only by listening to the future in a systematic way that scenarios become dynamic constructs that facilitate strategic dialog (see Listening as Practice: A Microsoft Story).

Scenarios must reflect the most current knowledge of the world through accurate research and reflection. More importantly, they must represent the best set of uncertainties so that organizations can chart their future by the best maps available. This combination of knowledge and uncertainty may be unsettling to people or organizations with low tolerance for ambiguity and/or a desire for confidence that outweighs concerns about risk. Scenarios, and processes for listening to the future, have proven to be a vigorous foundation for driving strategic dialog, and for crafting and executing informed actions.

Listening As Practice: A Microsoft Story

Microsoft decided in 2004 to actively explore the future of work in a radically different way. Rather than examining the future from the vantage point of existing products and current customer perceptions, Microsoft embarked on a scenario project that sought to frame the future workplace based on social, economic, political, and technological inputs.

In this quest to better understand its future (and everyone else's), Microsoft started with explorations around the future workforce. The company intuitively knew that the next generation of workers, the Millennials, was going to be different than members of the Baby Boom or Generation X. But they had far more exposure to the Baby Boom than any other generation, and the majority of information workers still fall into this cohort. In addition, much of the research conducted by product groups was focused on understanding how people want to see technology evolve based on their experience with current technology, with only a cursory examination of the broader social, economic, and political environment into which the technology would be deployed. To better understand the future workforce, Microsoft simultaneously engaged a group of 17–24 year old college students in a dialog about the future, and they also generated their own scenarios based on the focal question: *What will work look like in 2015?*

In June of 2004, the Microsoft Information Worker Business Group embarked on what has been a continuing journey to understand the next generation of workers through a program called the Microsoft Office Information Worker Board of the Future.[1] The inaugural board drew fifteen students from ten different countries. Upon their arrival at Microsoft's Redmond, WA campus, the students were quickly introduced to each other through an exercise that had them explore their past by posting their personal and technological experiences over the last ten years on long timelines taped to conference room walls. The IW Board was also asked to forecast events they foresaw over the next ten years. This exercise was designed from the outset to make sure that the Board members were focused on how their attitudes and thoughts would affect the future.

Following this ice-breaking exercise, the IW Board was engaged in a traditional scenario planning effort in which they were asked to describe the uncertainties related to the future of work, derive driving forces, and develop a matrix of possible futures.

What became clear from the first Board of the Future was the need for follow-on work. In 2005 Microsoft recruited another group of young people and continued the dialog about the future. In order to make effective use of time and drive toward meaningful results, the Microsoft team and the students focused on two very important issues:

1. What were the attitudes of the Millennials toward work and the underlying drivers for those attitudes?
2. How education could better prepare students for the workplace.

The results were clear recommendations about what individuals should be doing, what technology suppliers should be doing, and what society should be doing to prepare for the 1.5 billion Millennials who will join the workforce, and eventually lead the organizations that employ them.

The Board of the Future in isolation was insufficient, as it set no context for how the listening exercise would be applied. Microsoft developed its own scenarios immediately following the 2004 Board of the Future event to create a framework for strategic conversations, product planners and marketing leaders from within the Information Worker Business Groups were joined by representatives from Windows, MSN, and by Microsoft's internal Workplace Advantage Team, which is responsible for how Microsoft's physical office space will evolve.

The scenario process was fairly typical. The participants identified over 85 potential drivers and narrowed them down to 24. Four scenarios then emerged from the intersection of uncertainties around the pace and shape of the global economy (an open global economy or the reemergence of local, bordered states, and markets) and the way organizations would evolve (either maintaining a hierarchical view of the world, or embracing an organic, networked organizing principle).

Unlike many scenario planning efforts that age rapidly once they produce their initial set of robust implications, Microsoft maintains its scenarios through on-going dialogs with customers, through marketing and product exercises, and through active listening to the future. This dynamic process helps them continuously refine their assumptions by grinding the frameworks against emergent events and real experiences, and in so doing,

(continued)

keeps them well-honed to provide decision makers with up-to-the-minute insights into the real risks and opportunities that lie ahead.

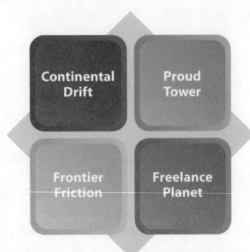

Microsoft's scenarios have changed the dynamic with many customers through their interaction with the robust implications now known as the *New World of Business*. The scenarios create a platform for discussion of uncertainties with customers and partners, and a framework for discussing data about globalization, the impact of technology on the workplace, the dynamics of the workforce, and the opportunities for transparency in light of the need for regulatory compliance.

EXPOSING THE DYNAMIC UNCERTAINTY LOOP

Several methods for making sense of incoming data and placing it into a strategic context are outlined in Listening as Practice: A Microsoft Story. Those methods work independently to make scenarios more sensitive to the dynamics of modern organizations and the environments they exist in. When combined into a dynamic uncertainty model, the various techniques can work systematically to reinforce themselves and reduce recurring costs associated with resources dedicated to scenario monitoring.

When the scenario team embarked on creating the next version of Microsoft's immersive future work experience called the Center for Information Work (CIW), the issue of data storage became a key element of the story, and it proved impossible to converge on an answer. The dilemma focused on how an unconscious patient's medical records would be retrieved in the future.

As the CIW crafted its new story, an unconscious character became part of the storyline. Arguments ensued about how this patient's medical history would be called up from the hospital's system. One suggestion: a USB drive on a keychain. Easy, but it could be lost. Also, highly likely, the records would be encrypted so a token would be required to access the records. No problem—biometrics would allow doctors to decrypt the files using a fingerprint to retinal scan. We complicated the story. Fingers severed, eyes damaged. Gory, but not implausible. And then there was the issue of permission and privacy. If the patient was unconscious, and the records were held privately, how would the institution know that they had permission to decrypt the files? What else might be encrypted beyond medical records? We then imagined a medical record clearance code. Like digital military tags, these artifacts would only be used for medical records, and if you had one, and were injured, then any institution could read the records, perhaps using a public, but restricted, key used just in these cases.

That was only part of the story, others argued. The records would be held in a central system and accessible from anywhere by any institution. Issues of permission and privacy still came up, as unconsciousness was a critical deterrent to determination of intent. But again, we crafted public policy on the fly. Missing body parts still held many at bay as the identification of the patient came into question.

Both situations were plausible, but neither was determined to be better than the other. What was critical here, from the uncertainty standpoint, was that neither situation solved the problem. As we added various aspects to the case, both could work, and both would fail, so there was likely a development that was beyond our imagination that would solve this problem, or the problem itself was truly intractable now, and potentially in the future. No matter the reason, it was clear that where private information was stored, how it was accessed, and how it was shared would remain an uncertainty within the decade covered by our scenarios, as would the trust models associated with access to personal information.

Monitoring Critical Uncertainties

This case aligns with the process titled *Monitoring Critical Uncertainties.* Beyond the tracking of information that pertains to the "official" uncertainties, this virtual team also watches for dynamic uncertainties, most of which surface as a story elements that cannot be easily reconciled with a whitepaper, video script, or a prototype narrative being crafted from the scenarios. If a new uncertainty meets the test of being robust across scenarios, adds additional information to the scenarios that potentially affect their outcomes, or enriches the story in a new and innovative way, it is adopted as part of the "official" uncertainty set.

The Center for Information Work case is but one example. Microsoft's scenarios on the future of information work have been widely shared, and active work has been conducted to create a community around the scenarios (of which this book is a part). Inputs come from Microsoft partners and customers worldwide. The volume is not high, but the insights are astute and the observations pointed. These customer interactions often bear out negative cases for dynamic uncertainties. For some examples of strategies derived from these conversations, see The Application of Insights.

One such challenge to the scenarios is their lack of first-glance recognition of security issues. How people store their identity or various other security issues were seen as peripheral to the scenario sets by the team that developed them. Although security was important, its importance was not uncertain in any potential future. Each of the scenarios reflected radically different models for security. From the standpoint of creativity, security is a fruitful topic to explore within the scenario set. Security, or the need for it, however, was not uncertain at all. At the level of the focal question about the future of work, people in the workforce would use some sort of security method to authenticate themselves, authorize their access and protect assets. How they did that did not change their work experience in a substantial way, so even though security processes in the future were unknown, security itself was known, and therefore failed the test as a critical uncertainty within the context of the future of work.

The Application of Insights

CHARACTER OF COMPETITION

Competition is often seen as an environmental constant in the market. Organizations act out of the imperative to compete successfully; the overarching motivation for the whole enterprise of strategic planning is usually motivated by the desire to create a future where the organization enjoys a greater competitive advantage than it does in the present.

Scenarios offer a unique way of viewing these competitive positioning battles by creating a set of stories that exist independently of the competitive dynamic. Although the future actions and state of competition can be played out against the scenarios, the scenarios themselves may be relatively unperturbed by the outcome of a single market. This can help put

(continued)

competitive dynamics into a new, more emotionally neutral ground that allows for more reasoned exposition of cause and effect against a background of uncertainty that is external to the incumbent, the competitor, or even the market. For example, if an oil company engaged in a scenario planning exercise that only took into account the internal dynamics of the oil market and its competitive landscape, the company might risk missing the possibility of changes outside the market—for example, the development of new sources of energy—that would make the company's relative position within the oil market unimportant.

Speed, agility, and adaptability are outcomes from futures-oriented processes and practices that organizations hope to achieve. Of these, speed is decisive. Adapting too late and finding all the new niches filled with experienced competitors, as evolutionary biologists will tell you, may be as detrimental as not adapting at all.

If the listening efforts yield a positive result, then they should provide an organization with ample time to adapt relative to competitors. However, speed is not inherent in the process. Only through **system trust** does speed manifest itself. Organizations often don't extend trust to processes they can't measure, or methodologies that don't produce consistent outcomes from transparent reproducible processes. By its nature, the scenario planning process is neither entirely consistent and nor entirely transparent. Different exercises with different participants will yield different results. Forecasts may be useful in a lot of little ways but wrong in big, unmistakable ones.

How much trust would policy makers extend to forecasters whose scenarios in the mid-1980s didn't include at least the possibility of a collapse of Communism, or software companies in the early '90s who simply could not envision any kind of large-scale data network except for private, proprietary ones? The answer is probably "more than you might think." Even good scenario planning will often fail miserably in retrospect. Classic works of respected futurists are littered with embarrassing blown calls.

Unlike many typical management practices, scenario planning must be judged more on its process than its outcome, at least initially. Over time, the advantages of taking a systematic and disciplined approach to scenario planning will become evident. The introduction of dynamic uncertainties can enhance trust because the models never become stale artifacts, but rather reflect current realities of question, along with long-standing uncertainties. The act of dialog facilitated by scenarios stimulates thinking that can lead, perhaps indirectly, to positive insights, actions, and outcomes that will simply be taken for granted as "good business decisions." Managers should learn to recognize and perhaps even document these good effects of scenario planning as a way of investing the process itself with greater rigor. Rigor will lead to trust. And once there is trust in the planning process, organizations can act on the outputs of robust scenario planning exercises with speed and confidence.

Managing complexity therefore becomes an outcome of scenarios, and by the nature of managed uncertainty, places limitations on what is listened to. By focusing on important uncertainties, organizations create a manageable set of external factors to monitor that complement internal metrics by providing a context for those metrics. Rather than looking at metrics in isolation, metrics can become part of the overall listening process by linking key performance indicators to the scenarios.

It is normative practice to examine an organization from a single point of view at a single point in time (and within the context of some goal for a future state against which it is being evaluated). Placing performance indicators in the context of scenarios creates a means for evaluating those indicators for their directional vectors, both in terms of the directionality of global or regional developments *vis-à-vis* the scenarios, as well as the evolution of the performance metrics themselves. Over time, as the background of the scenarios shifts, the performance indicators of the organization may need to adapt to the emergent strategic realities.

Overall, scenarios and the listening process help manage complexity through context. Some may argue that by increasing the amount of data, and certainly expanding the scope well beyond internally controlled variables, complexity increases. But it can also be argued that internal metrics without context create more complexity as causal relationships become more difficult to discern against effects as they expand outside the boundaries of the organization. By mapping key performance indicators against scenarios and using them as a means to enhance the fidelity of the listening exercise, an organization can see that its own complexity becomes dwarfed by the larger context. For those charged with scenario management, linking performance indicators can provide a means of linking the sometimes-abstract narratives to operational measures, and therefore

(continued)

grounding them in a language and a reality that resonates better with the organization.

Organizational intent is often difficult to place if an organization does not create transparency in its strategic planning process. Acquisitions, emphasis or de-emphasis of products or process, staffing choices, and other actions that are taken without the context of scenarios, and the results of listening activities, can appear random or uninformed. By linking action to the rich backdrop of scenarios as well as the results of listening exercises, organizations can not only make better informed decisions, but can better communicate those decisions as the external and internal logic combine to reinforce the compelling business value—and perhaps even the emotional impact—of a business decision.

Not all decisions are based in clear logic and sound reason; some are, in fact, emotionally based. Scenarios and their rich stories create a natural means for drawing deep connections to strategic action that inform organizational intent.

Organizational culture is difficult to move. Storytelling advocate Stephen Denning, former Director of Knowledge Management at the World Bank, sees stories as the best means to obtaining meaningful and lasting shifts in culture. Because both scenarios and the listening process create stories, they move away from abstractions and create more concrete illustrations of strategic intent, and therefore offer management a means for moving culture through inspiration and aspiration.

Financial bandwidth does not expand in light of listening exercises, but it can become a part of the overall equation of action when managed in light of competitive analysis, organizational intent, and other factors discussed here. Budgets, much like other actions created without transparent context, can be more easily refined, and their alignment more easily communicated, by aligning them with scenarios and the results of listening. Budget should be tied to organizational intent, and although this is intuitive and would seem a best practice, it is neither.

If context for organizational intent is unclear, then associated budgets are also unclear—not in absolute terms, but in terms of magnitude and distribution against organizational objectives. Stating clearly what the organization is watching and what it is investing in based on robust implications and contingencies, turns budgets into reinforcements of organizational intent rather than additional points of confusion for managers.

ACTING ON WHAT YOU HEAR

Listening to the future is of little consequence if the insights gained are not heeded as part of an overall strategic dialog about direction. It is often difficult for those exposed to scenario thinking to place far-flung hypotheticals into practical action. But it is essential that this be done. Well-drawn scenarios offer decision-makers clear choices based on futures with distinctive, obvious attributes. Once those attributes have been identified, management is empowered to take actions that either take advantage of insights derived from scenarios thus finding opportunity for growth, or they hedge against them, and therefore protect the organization from risk. Either action is appropriate and uses sense-making about the future in a way that informs action.

It must be reinforced, however, that simply *taking action on first findings is dangerous*, and the techniques outlined in *Listening to the Future* are intended to demonstrate the value of scenario planning as an ongoing, dynamic process that produces increasingly refined and actionable results with successive iterations. Organizations that run a scenario planning exercise then take the initial findings as a permanent and unchanging mandate for action will quickly lose the benefits of their investment in foresight and perhaps become disenchanted with the process, leaving them even less equipped to deal with future challenges.

The following recommendations suggest ways in which listening to the future can be used by an organization to strengthen strategy, enhance innovation, and drive thought leadership.

Strengthening strategy: All of these techniques are designed at the first order for one purpose: to strengthen strategy. If they do not inform an organization's plans, actions, positions, or perspectives, then they are tools that should not be engaged. For those that do embrace the power of these techniques, they gain a twofold benefit. The first is in creating frameworks for internal and external strategic conversations that do not constrain their options in the present, but that challenge employees, managers, partners, and customers to take a broader view of future possibilities. The scenarios present the organization with creative venues for identifying new opportunities that would remain hidden had they not ventured into potential futures that differ from the "official" future or forecast. The energy and inquiry spurred by this process itself can drive benefits such as operational

(continued)

innovations, workforce motivation, and a market reputation for thought-leadership that adds value to the brand.

Second, the techniques for listening to the future provide new organizational sensing mechanisms that increase the bandwidth of an organization. They are akin to using infrared night goggles to enhance vision, or examining the cosmos through microwaves or radio. These techniques reveal hidden data. Perhaps most importantly, though, it is not the hidden data, but the hidden patterns that best inform strategy. The framework creates a lattice work upon which an organization can hang its findings and map relationships against those findings.

Enhancing innovation: One of the best ways to position strategically is to take a leading position in a product, process, or service area. Listening to the future can enhance innovation by providing insight into the goods and services that will be required in the future. Innovations may be powerfully contingent in that the identification of an opportunity may depend on uncertainties. Organizations must use their enhanced sensing capabilities to align anticipation and action. While listening to the future, organizations may well identify innovative ideas, but those ideas may exist prematurely to the world that will adopt them and make them successful. By using early warning signs, for instance, organizations can place innovations within the context of future action, with the early warning system acting as the trigger for action.

Taking the high ground: Although Microsoft's scenarios were used internally for windtunneling new products and strategies, and questioning assumptions about their markets, they have become more of a backdrop for the possibilities customers need to understand about how work will evolve. As a proof point for vision, the scenarios create a context for strategic conversations with customers and partners at a level that focuses not on the impact of individual technologies, or even suits of technology, but in the goals of the technology within the context of business need. With the New World of Work as derivative of the scenarios, and with active data collection and ongoing dialog focused on listening to the future, the scenarios create enhanced credibility for deep dialogs about how technology will affect business in a world of increasing globalization and transparency, and against which technology and demographics are reshaping the workplace itself.

Cocreating the Future

The work with communities is bidirectional. While Microsoft shares its scenarios in an effort to further refine its insights, it also shares its insights from a unique perspective as the representative of a 550-million active user base within today's workplace. Microsoft is uniquely positioned to ask questions about the future of work in a meaningful way that can act as a catalyst for discussion across industries. The scenarios, as represented in the New World of Work, have been presented to hundreds of Microsoft customers, each of whom is invited to become a part of the extended community that thinks about the evolution of the workplace. This has evolved over the last several years, from a communication exercise to a time management exercise as more and more customers request to participate in this dialog. One significant customer in banking, for instance, has used the New World of Work and the scenarios as guidelines for their own corporate reinvention, with Microsoft engaged as an active partner in the transformation of their retail and investment banking services.

Ambassadors of the Future

The Microsoft Office Information Worker Board of the Future has already been discussed, but their influence as "ambassadors of the future" goes well beyond the structured learning exercises conducted while they were directly engaged in the events or their participation as members of a community aware of our scenarios. Many of the outcomes from the Board of the Future have acted as critical inputs to education strategy and thought leadership on understanding of the next generation workplace. This ambassadorial learning connects Microsoft directly with representatives of the future workforce, engages with them in an ongoing way so that opinions expressed, as they might be in a focus group, become tangible and real learning as the engagement continues over a course of years.

The Board of the Future has taught the keen lessons reflected at the beginning of this article about trends. Despite seemingly overwhelming evidence of generalized and unified behavior by the Millennial generation with regard to work, the generation itself, while behaving much as trends predict, remains cautious about future behavior in light of potential disruptive events.

In the early days of knowledge management, the looming reality of aging Baby Boomers was a recurrent theme. From government to banking to oil exploration, organizations feared the loss of knowledge stored in the heads of their most experienced employees. Because knowledge management was seldom scenario-based, practitioners failed to think about the next generation in a different way. As with much traditional planning, the next generation workforce was seen as an extension of the current workforce, and therefore, as the repository for this knowledge.

If the knowledge management profession had been *listening to the future*, they would have imagined, perhaps, that the next generation may not necessarily be interested in perpetuating the knowledge of the past. New industries, reactions against corporate crime, and massive distrust sowed by layoffs and offshoring, may create a generation that is more entrepreneurial—one that seeks disruption to some extent, rather than continuity.

That later characterizations have become standard to descriptions of the Millennial generation in developed countries. Thus the uncertainty associated with generations is much more about the interactions between them, rather than how the Millennials will engage the workplace, or if the Baby Boomers will retire or not. GenX is a wild card, as their cynicism and skepticism may make them poor managers for either the ambitious, socially responsible, and technology–savvy Millennials, or the newly empowered Boomers, who once released from the shackles of a traditional workplace may act more like Millennials as they reenter the workforce. This intergenerational situation is, of course, much more complex than this brief profile suggests, but it clearly exposes critical uncertainties that go beyond a traditional bipolar axis toward complex and blurry uncertainties defined by their interplay rather than their independence.

All of these inputs create the potential for dynamic uncertainties. Dynamic uncertainties require a regular review of their impact on scenarios, rather than the traditional "batch" mode of scenario planning which revisits scenario sets occasionally over a five-year period, if at all. Dynamic uncertainties are only valuable if the scenarios are actively managed and used regularly to drive strategic dialog.

Over the course of its scenario development and management, Microsoft has garnered significant insights, including:

- Scenarios and the active engagement of customer communities in the process over time can reinforce or establish thought leadership integrity, and create a platform for ongoing learning.
- Scenarios with a single focal question can be effectively repurposed to other uses if they are sufficiently generalized in their description. The future of work scenarios, given their broad global perspective, have been used as the basis for the exploration of questions ranging from branding to software, from public policy to hardware design.
- Using scenarios as a framework for learning creates a strong feedback loop that helps identify emergent behavior.

Dynamic uncertainties significantly enhance the credibility of scenarios by creating a platform for living stories that connect more readily to the emergent situations customers and employees face, rather than static scenarios that run the risk of becoming artifacts with diminishing relevance over time.

FINDING THE SIGNAL IN THE NOISE

Microsoft embraced this more dynamic adaptation of scenario planning methodology because of its unique position in an industry that is on the cutting edge of change. Software development moves at a pace that many other commercial activities do not, or at least did not, until recently. As global integration and connectivity intensify competitive pressure in all industries and challenge all organizations to take quick measure of their situation and adapt, Microsoft's experiences may be instructive.

Dynamic uncertainties are just one example of finding meaningful signals in the noise of information that surrounds us. Here are some of the others that Microsoft uses.

Research: In the Future of Information Work program, research is not constrained to trend-tracking, but rather is designed to look for changes in the margins of established trends. The research conducted on behalf of the Future of Work places every piece of third-party reporting into a forcibly *unbiased* framework before a kind of rigid bias is directly applied. In other words, we ask *to which future* (or futures) a particular story points, rather than seeing any report as a general pointer toward "the future." In this way, research becomes not an act in itself, but a part of the early-warning system (see below) which seeks to gather a preponderance of evidence for a particular future in order to expose the implications associated with that future.

Analyst reports: Information technology analysts fit a particular ecological niche when listening to the future. They are, for the most part, paid for their impartiality, but valued for their strong opinions. When used as part of a listening to the future exercise, analyst reports help test the extremes, as routinely they take their opinion in a single direction, and stake their reputations, over time, on the accuracy of their predictions.

These extreme positions can be valuable aids in guarding against bias. Once they are placed in the continuum of research, they act as a pole star for a particular point of view, defining one edge of the field of analysis. Unlike traditional reporting, which attempts to be unbiased, and thus forces the investigator to form his or her own opinion about the underlying motivation of the reporter, information technology analysis typically displays its bias in its headline, and then explores that point of view through deep causal underpinnings and primary research that acts to "prove the point."

In contrast to opinions found in newspapers, magazines, and blogs, those of information technology analysts, as well as financial analysts, avoid opinion for the sake of opinion (at least in theory), but rather build out their case through a more rigorous and informed process. It is in the underlying logic and uniquely informed (or experienced) perspective of the analyst that make these types of reports valuable beyond the five minutes it takes to read them. Since scenarios are stories about the future that have deep internal logics, the reports of analysts can not only point to extreme positions, but can also help provide part of the narrative that drives the story forward.

Early warning systems: Watchlist and trigger efforts cannot be fully automated. This is yet another example of the rapid ability of human beings to migrate toward the certain. By creating a search list in a tool like Factiva, the researcher is by default stating that the uncertainty has become certain in its definition, and therefore no longer a variable (or at least no longer interesting enough to watch for change in and of itself). By doing this, the researcher substitutes the certainty of assumption for the vigilance of the genuinely curious. The researcher places limits on the inputs and may inadvertently miss emergent uncertainties. To avoid this, any automated search method should be supplemented with extensive "page-turning" research that seeks to identify patterns that identify emergent uncertainties. Although this technique seems to suggest a removal of all limits, it is in fact always regulated by the focal question. The reader is searching not for *all* emergent uncertainties, but only for those pertaining to the question on which their scenarios are focused.

The late Harvard paleontologist Stephen Jay Gould was an advocate of rethinking evolutionary trends. He observed that it can be deceptive to focus on single factors for change rather than looking at the evolution of entire systems. The .400 batting average in baseball was a favorite of his, with his analysis showing its demise was not the fault of batters or the betterment of pitchers, but the result of an overall increase in the excellence of play[2].

Those listening to the future must also be wary of overinvesting in the meaning of specific trends. Too often today, many organizations reduce market trends to cute acronyms that may shield them from both threat and opportunity. An emerging classic is the marketing moniker of BRIC (Brazil, Russia, India and China). The formalization of this acronym is a sure sign that real thinking has stopped and been replaced with a convenient shorthand, while analysts proceed to construct towers of assumptions based on a "fact" whose predictive value has not been established. While we watch the BRIC countries (because analysts tell us we should), we risk missing the emergence of other places that may have more impact over time than these four countries (note the reshuffling of power in the Middle East or the reascendance of Marxism in Latin America, both of which are potentially disruptive events).

Anticipation webs: One outcome of developing ambassadors of the future is their inclusion in *anticipation webs*. Anticipation webs are social networks with the common bond of having been exposed to a certain set of scenarios, and creating an emotional attachment to those scenarios in ways that create a community of interest and action. These webs then act as an extended sensing mechanism for both the internal variables of the scenarios and those emergent events and trends that may perturb the logic of the models.

Future work role: Another way to gather insight into future workers is to have people imagine their roles, in a particular future, developing expansive questions that focus them on the experience of working in a particular scenario. Although this exercise is of particular interest to Microsoft and the question of how people will work in the future, similar investigations can be used by organizations to help their employers orient themselves within scenarios, expand the details of the scenarios, and create an emotional attachment to the scenarios that will be useful as the scenarios become used routinely.

New employee orientation: In order to gather insights into the idea of future work, Microsoft uses an exercise called New Employee Orientation. This exercise has attendees imagine what a New Employee Orientation looks like in 2015, with Baby Boomers rejoining the workforce from failed retirements or the search for meaning in a new line of work, sitting alongside Millennial employees on their fifth or sixth change in career trajectory, still much more defined by their lives outside of work than their life at work. What uncertainties does this conjure up? What are people thinking about the employer, their future, each other?

Windtunneling goes hand-in-hand with scenario planning. It is the practice of testing ideas and concepts against the logics of the scenarios. The term comes from automobile design, where colored smoke is blown over a model to see how the contours of a vehicle affect aerodynamics. Testing marketing plans, new products, or competitive responses within the context of the scenario's logics does much the same as the smoke in the windtunnel. You can think of your concept as interacting with the narrative of the scenario, the story flows around and through the concept. As you talk through this process, you want to be aware of all of the characters of your story (the uncertainties) and how the concept is changed by them, and how it affects them

Rapid prototyping/learning by doing: Internally-consistent logical models are excellent tools, but they should never be mistaken for reality. Real learning comes from direct evidence. Facts on the ground should displace suppositions at the earliest opportunity, and integrated into the planning process is an analogue to the industrial process of "rapid prototyping." As an illustration, consider the process that a company like HP would use to introduce a fundamental printing technology into the market. Because HP already has a mature market channel, the ability to gather and interpret customer data can rapidly inform their product development process. Rapid prototyping allows them to introduce products that refine an approach, as well as to incorporate early warning elements as customers start to uptake a new technology. Rapid feedback on prototypes can also act as an early indicator that a technology is immature, or that it is not going to be accepted for one reason or the other, including being ahead of its time relative to consumer need or other technologies. Organizations should use their connections to customers, the market, and other sources of evidence to constantly refine and validate their scenario model, and take the feedback they receive seriously.

LOOKING FORWARD

We have not yet invented perfect models for anticipating the future for organizations and probably never will. The variables are too vast. But there are methods that reveal more about the future, ways of reasoning about those characteristics, and most importantly, roles and methods that help an organization stay engaged with the future in a way that helps inform their strategic intent and guide their tactics and execution.

Although scenario planning creates a framework for an ongoing dialog about the future derived from uncertainties, it does not create a framework for the *ongoing examination* of the underlying uncertainties. Scenarios tend to be iterative in nature as they are revisited from time to time in their entirety. In the best cases, they evolve into a clearly articulated set of indicators that can be watched. They rarely become dynamic models of the future, more often being relegated to the role alongside probability engines. Highly probable futures distract people from plausible alternatives and tend to reinforce an "official future." In these situations, scenarios prove ineffective tools for challenging assumptions or managing contingencies and risk.

Listening to the future transforms scenarios into dynamic business partners. The titles of the scenarios can take on almost anthropomorphic characteristics. If we consider the markets that scenarios were designed to serve, such as its original application in the energy industry, the dynamics of that market in the 1950s and 1960s were slow, and uncertainties could be allowed to play out almost leisurely as the organizations contemplated the actions they would take in light of emerging clarity about those things previously found uncertain. As scenarios evolve into dynamic systems, they may prove more complex for organizations to manage, but the benefit will come in strategic models that account for the reduced half-life of change so visible in today's business climate.

NOTES

1. Daniel W. Rasmus, "Information Workers of the Future at Microsoft." *KM Review*, Chicago, Vol. 7, Issue 5 November/December 2005.
2. Stephen Jay Gould, *Full House: The Spread of Excellence from Plato to Darwin*. New York, Three Rivers Press, 1996.

W hat should a software company say about the future of business and work?

That's one of the questions that Dan Rasmus sought to answer when he left his role as Research Vice President for Forrester Research to join Microsoft in 2003 as Director for Information Work Vision. Microsoft was the driving force in the information work revolution that began in the 1980s with the first wave of PCs and office applications, then accelerated as the Internet redefined communications channels, customer relationships, and business models in the 1990s. The centrality of information technology (IT) to business transformation was inescapably clear, yet in many cases, Microsoft was still perceived simply as a software vendor. Strategic discussions were largely confined to IT departments and procurement managers, whose traditional metrics were increasingly inadequate to represent the true business value of new technologies in the connected workplace.

Dan and the senior management of the Microsoft Business Division felt it was important to raise the level of dialog to address issues facing business decision makers, above and beyond the usual conversations about IT benefits. The company conducted a series of structured planning sessions to incorporate a wide range of perspectives on the future of work and business, taking the broadest possible view of technology in the context of social, political, economic, and demographic developments. In 2005, then-Microsoft Chairman Bill Gates delivered a keynote address on "The New World of Work," which formalized the vision and laid out many of the ideas that Dan would develop through further discussions with customers.

Dan engaged Rob Salkowitz, a strategic consultant and business writer, to help articulate the themes that emerged from the planning

sessions and the ongoing research in a series of white papers published from 2005 to the present, each addressing a particular facet
of the business conversation. The first iteration of this process produced four approaches to the future of work: One World of Business;
Always On, Always Connected; Transparent Organizations; and Workforce Evolution. These were collected, along with Managing Knowledge
in the New World of Work, in a special-order edition of this book,
originally titled *Listening to the Future: Insights from the New World of
Work.*

In the meantime, Microsoft continued to explore the implications of
the driving forces of social and technological change, this time from the
perspective of the top priorities facing business leaders. Given a world
that is Always On and Always Connected, how do businesses derive
insights from the complexities of an environment that is saturated by
information? How do businesses adapt to the ever-changing edges of
everything from workforce boundaries to the perceived value of intellectual property and still succeed in such a blended world? How do global
businesses—which is to say, nearly all businesses today—stay agile and
dynamic in an era of new relationships, new business models, and rising
expectations of consumers? And finally, how does IT act as the strategic foundation that enables and empowers a business's workforce and
partners to quickly adapt?

This revised edition of *Listening to the Future* collects the latest strategic insights from Microsoft, and presents them alongside the earlier material to present an inclusive picture of Microsoft's current thinking. We
have provided new material to add context and summarized a series of
papers written for individual industries to show how the New World of
Business themes filter down to the specific priorities faced by manufacturers, financial service companies, governments, professional service
firms, retailers, and others. Because each white paper was originally
meant to stand alone, there is some inevitable repetition of core principles, which we hope in this case will serve to reinforce the main themes
and ideas. The final chapter describes the scenario planning method in
depth and offers guidance for organizations that want to apply this same
kind of structured analysis to their own organization.

No single individual, no one organization, no nation or even group of nations can successfully navigate the changes ahead. This book intends to create a dialog with customers and policymakers about how to best apply our resources and capabilities to the challenges ahead. Organizations that succeed will find that listening to the future, and turning insight into action, truly is everybody's business.

Index